High Shelf

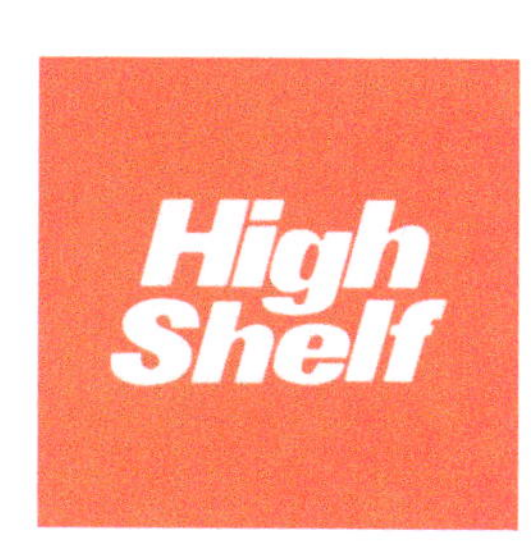

High Shelf XXVI, January 2021.
Portland, Oregon.
Copyright 2021, High Shelf Press

Paperback ISBN: 978-1-952869-23-5

Cover Image by Turner Hilliker
Design and Layout by C. M. Tollefson
Editing by David Seung & C. M. Tollefson

With special thanks to:
Kelsey Beck Kuther, Megan Kim, & River Elizabeth Hall.

High Shelf XXVI

January 2021

"I remember when you became atoms

Sparsed into binary switches
On—off—black—white
That allowed space in your body
To breathe.

I remember when you found your shadow..."
Brandyce Ingram

"...No church-shelter for us, burdened one,
We are more the sentinels at the ford,
unsure of our own footing, march-weary,
hoping our words will somehow see us through..."
Ciarán Ó Gríofa

Table Of Contents

"Coming Down"   9
        Andy Kerstetter
nature's curtain   10
        Sarah Bricault
Sanguine   11
        Chris Foster
Lillie Lemon   12
        Laurie Philip Michaels
Body   20
        Emily Benson
Letter to a Ghost   21
        Brandyce Ingram
Chicago Quarantined   22
        Michelle Geoga
Why this is the best time to see your ex   30
        Clara Mendoza
Food Chain   31
        Paul Ilechko
No Sanctuary.   33
        Ciarán Ó Gríofa
Dialogue   34
        Turner Hilliker
Anthropocene Fire Gardens   48
        Ann-Marie Brown
Invitations   58
        Taylor Mallay
The Art of Piercing   60
        Rommel Chrisden Rollan Samarita
Circus Girl   61
        Kat Hofland
Living in a White World   62
        Chad Murray
Art Submission   67
        Jason R. Montgomery

A Dangerous Game 72
Lily Rooks
Donuts at the Fair, and the Banality of a Sweet Tooth 73
Will McDonald
Ekphrastic Challenge 78
Andrea Jones & Sonya Burke

"Coming Down"

Andy Kerstetter

Excuse me, Captain, I'd like to get off
this plane—pardon me while I pack up
    my neuroses, eagle-feathered
shamans sardined in my sealskin
    sack of forget-me-
nots, plucked from the meadow in the back
    of my throat even as
    they wither on my tongue.

    Bring us down gently
in that city of bladed hills, gleaming
    like the cigarette glow
reflected in his eyes, ashes
    falling—like our worst intentions
    —over everything.

    Please don't leave
me in that flyover country, checkered with grids
    of blooming apple trees, rows
and rows of white petals swaying
    like pearl necklaces
discarded by widowed heiresses
    spending their fortunes on their own
        private islands.

But before you let me out on this tarmac
    paved with all my stillborn
promises, give me a moment
    to shred these mushrooms
sprouting from the crown
    of my head.

nature's curtain

Sarah Bricault

The skull, the carapace of the mind,
is an architectural marvel,
a fusion of plates that curve
towards each other. When they meet,
bits of bone twine together
like fingers, like puzzle pieces,
making a solid seal. But the proof
of distinction remains, beneath
layers of skin and hair. It is
enthralling, how even nature hides her
growing pains, her battle scars. We
can only see the beauty of formation
after flesh has fallen away. Or,
if we peer into the womb, note that
fetal features betray her thinking,
evolution obvious from the bird-like,
frog-like offspring before it shapes itself
human. It reminds me that I too have been shaped
from myself, many times, but that
transformation does not always require
that I cease living and turn to goo
— no offense, butterfly —
but can be the kind of gradual growth
that the body undergoes as those
plates of bone become one. And perhaps
nature is wrong, in this, in hiding
what has come before — and perhaps
that is the lesson. If I can run my fingers
down ridges of bone and marvel at the eons
that created them, if I can peer past
nature's curtain and love her all the more
for it — perhaps there is someone out there
who could feel the same
about me.

Sanguine

Chris Foster

She moves like Zinfandel
when afternoon lowers its gaze
upon the earth

the red hills
outside the city sway gently
into her bare thighs

shadows
find evening in the rhythm
of her feet

in the silhouette
of her shape upon the sky

the stars
come out to please her
with their silver dust

with their distant music
offered like candles
to her concert

bedsheets
summoned to her body
as subjects

and I
as small as the stars
as common as the sky

I kneel
in her sanguine
and wait

Lillie Lemon

Laurie Philip Michaels

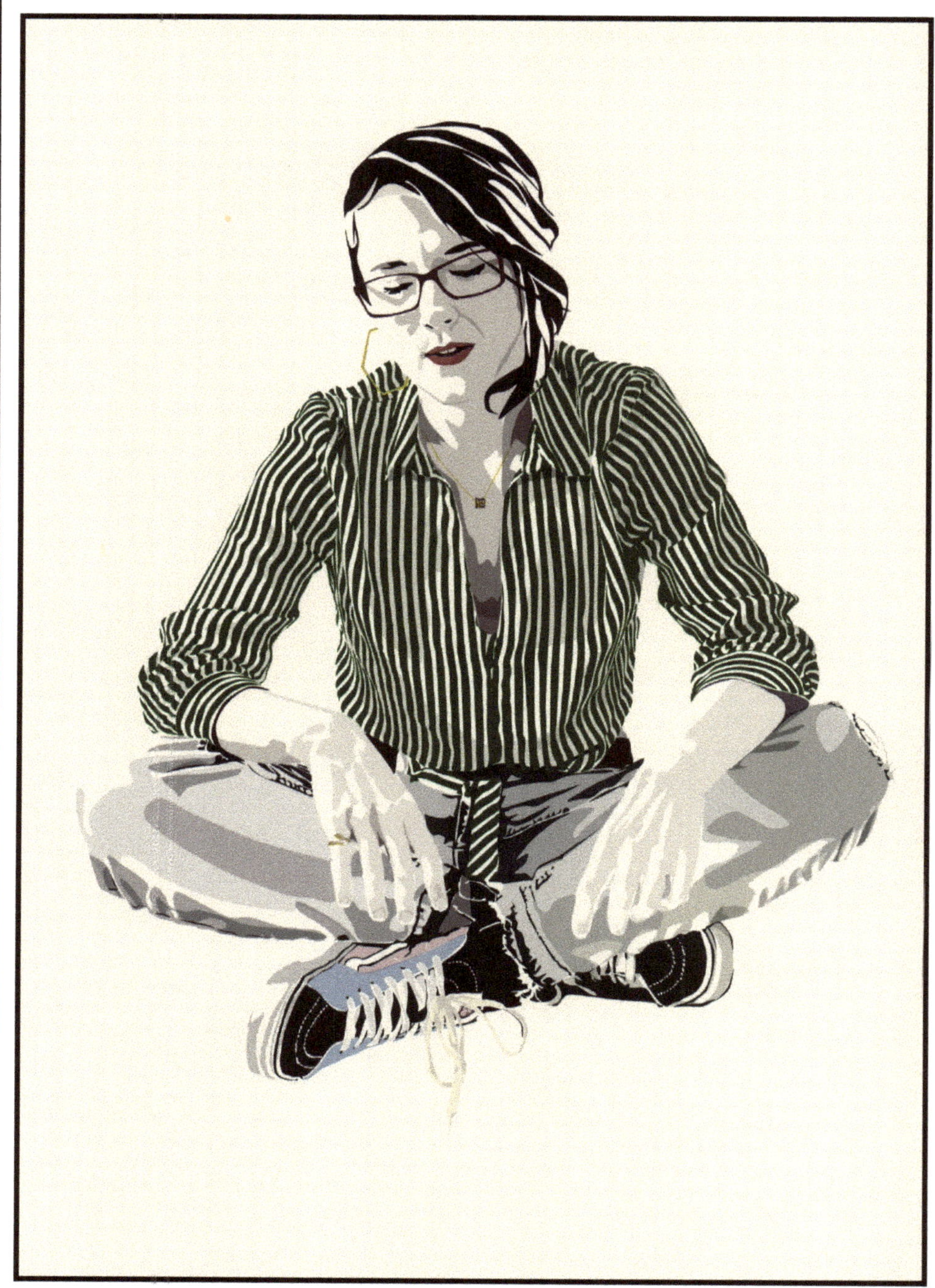

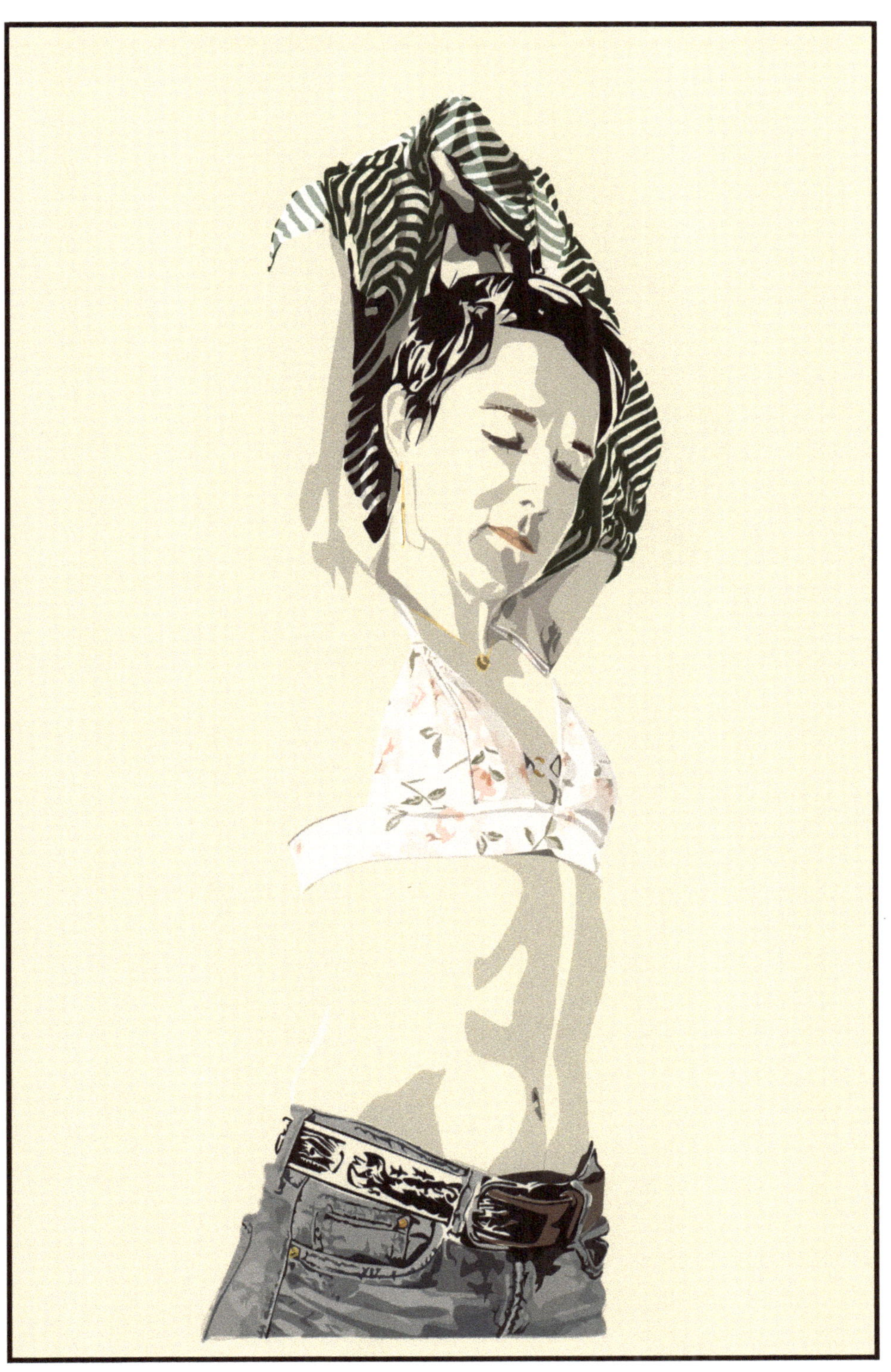

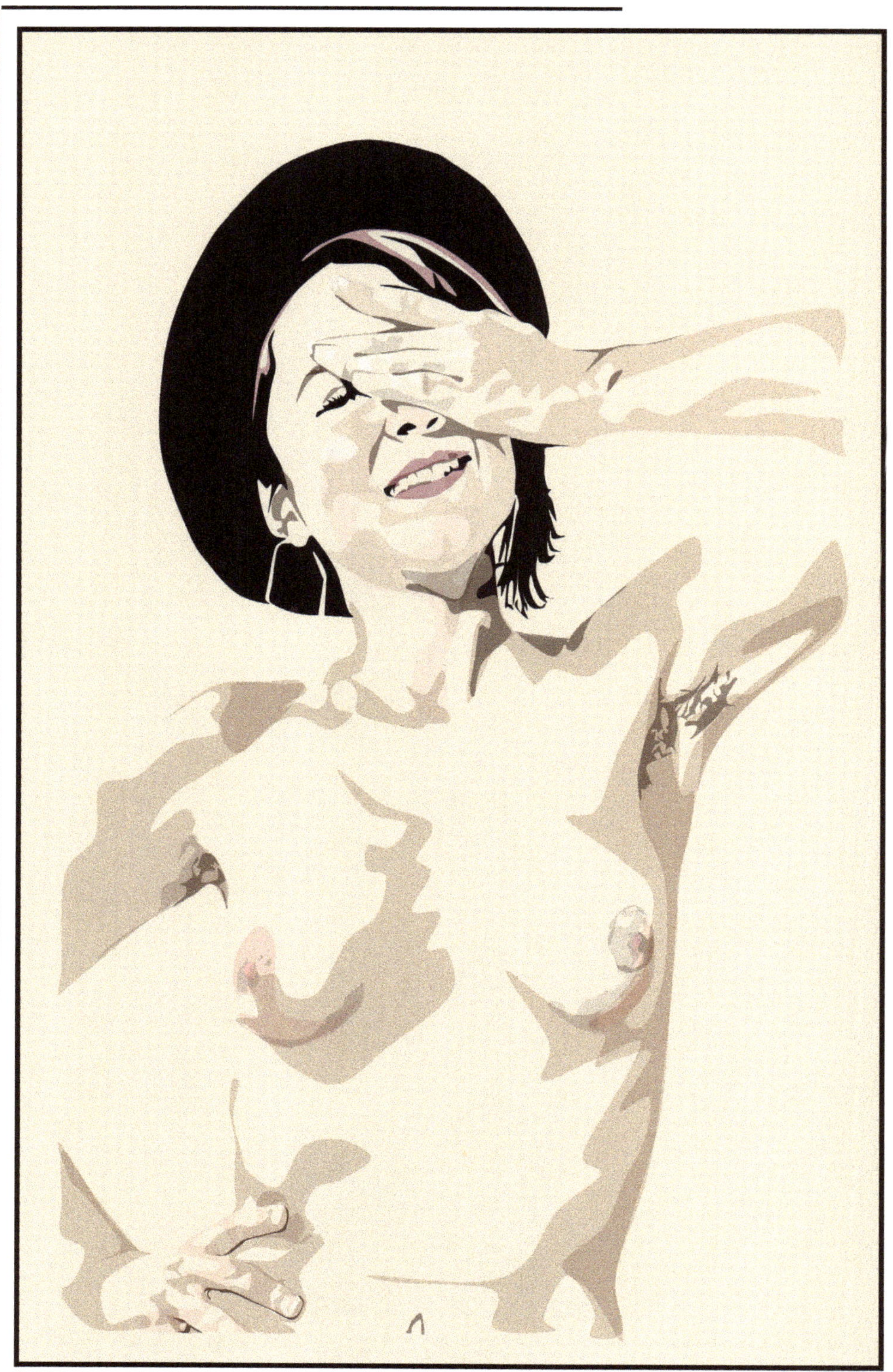

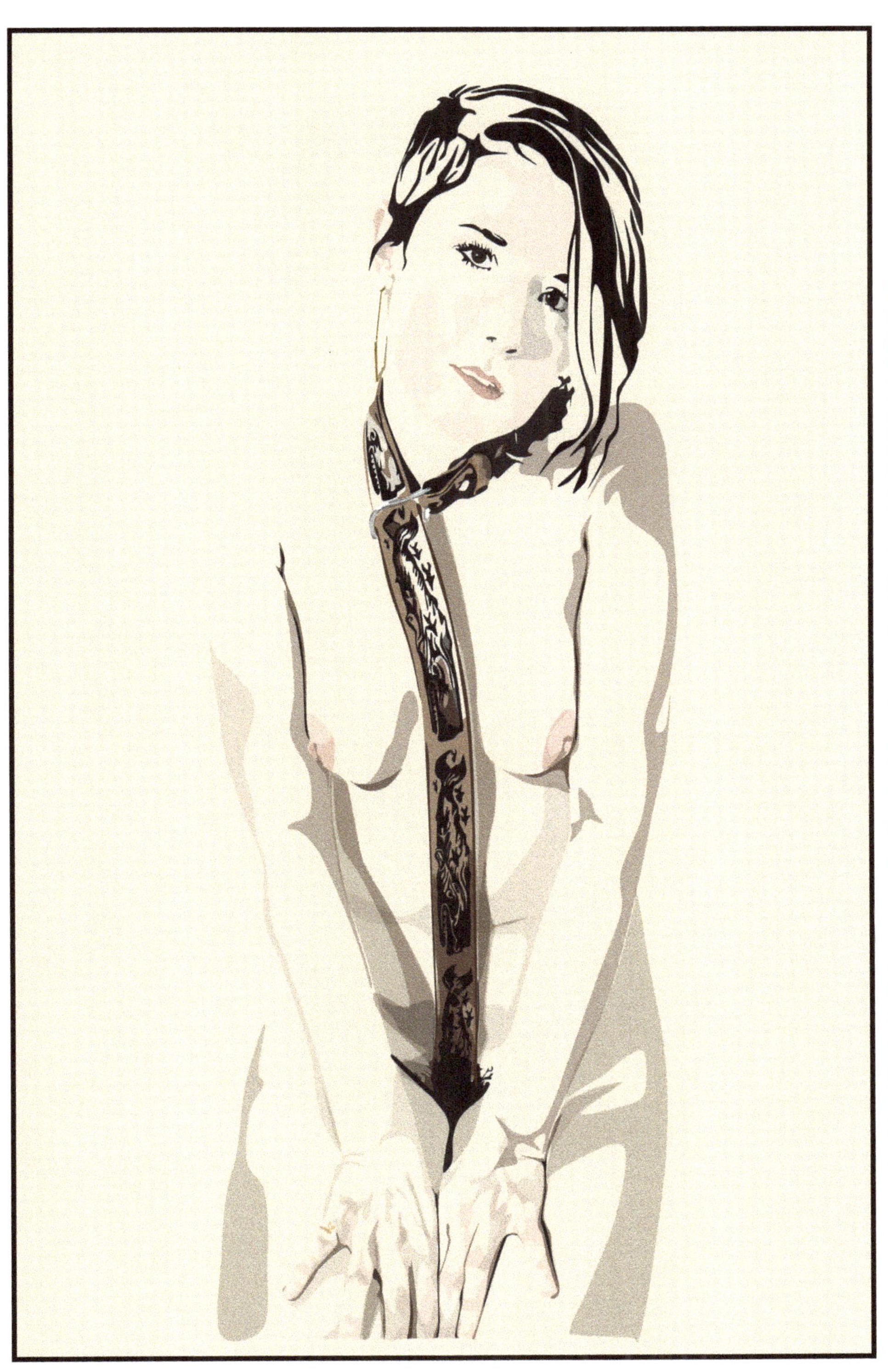

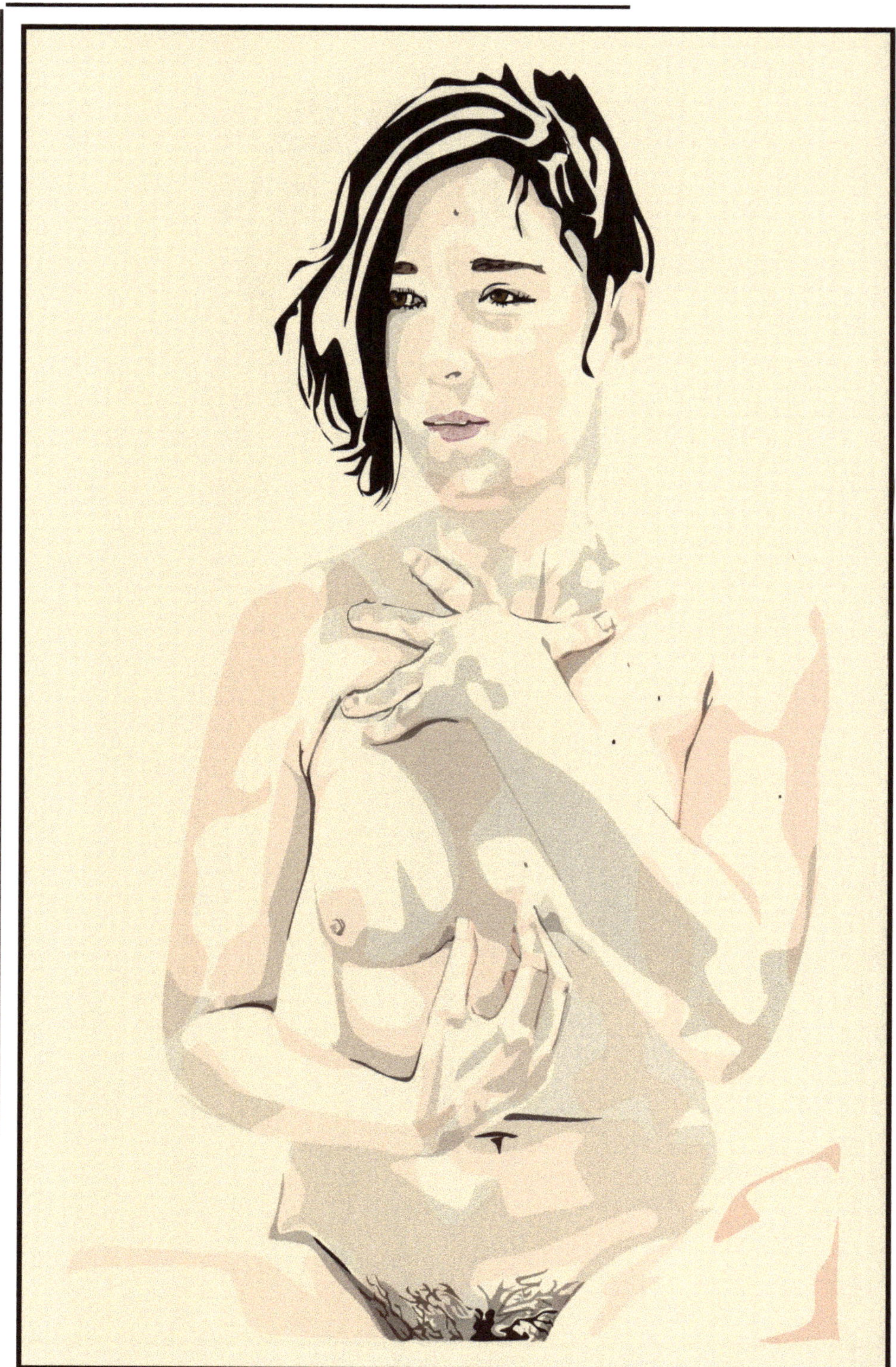

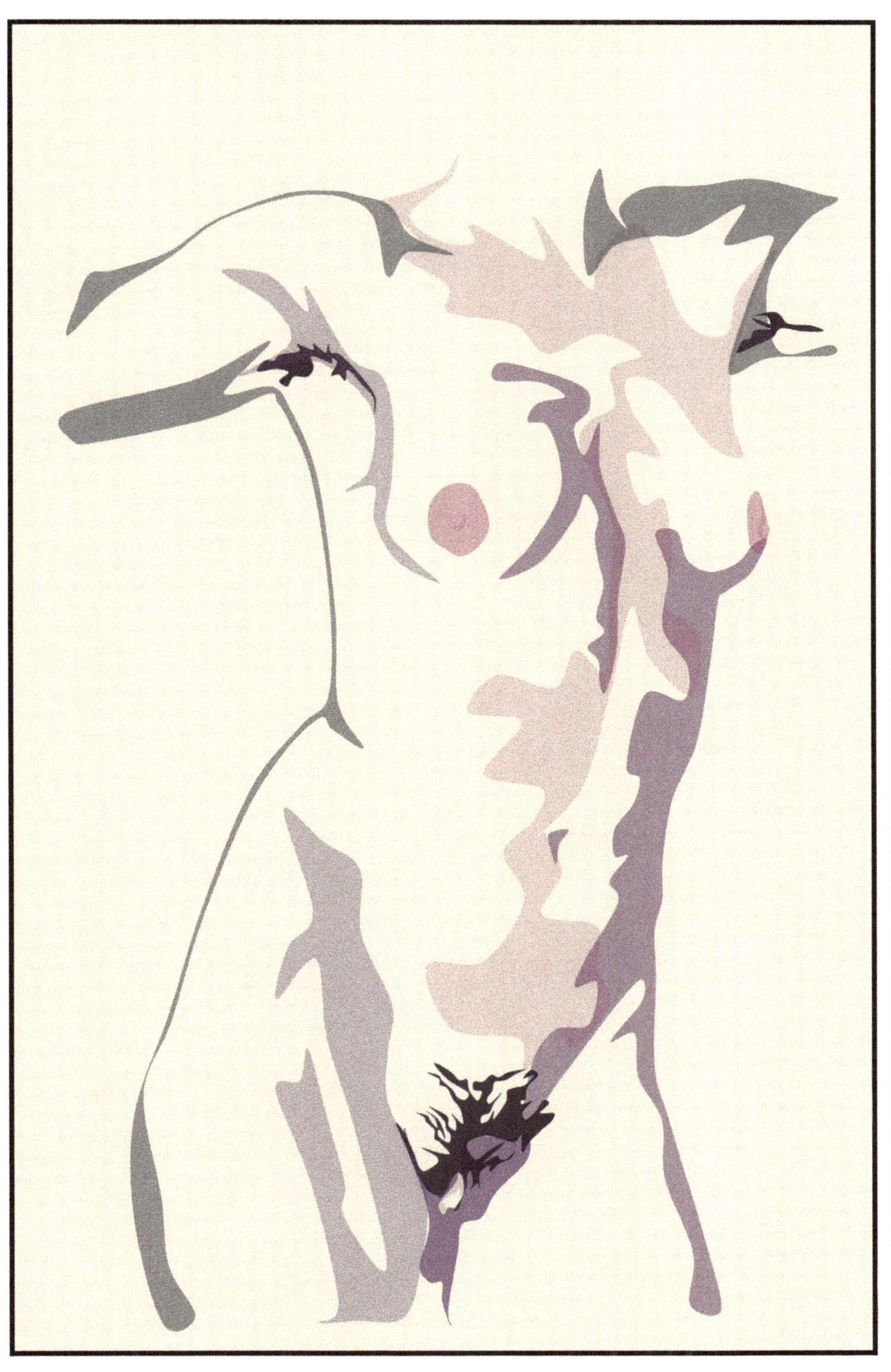

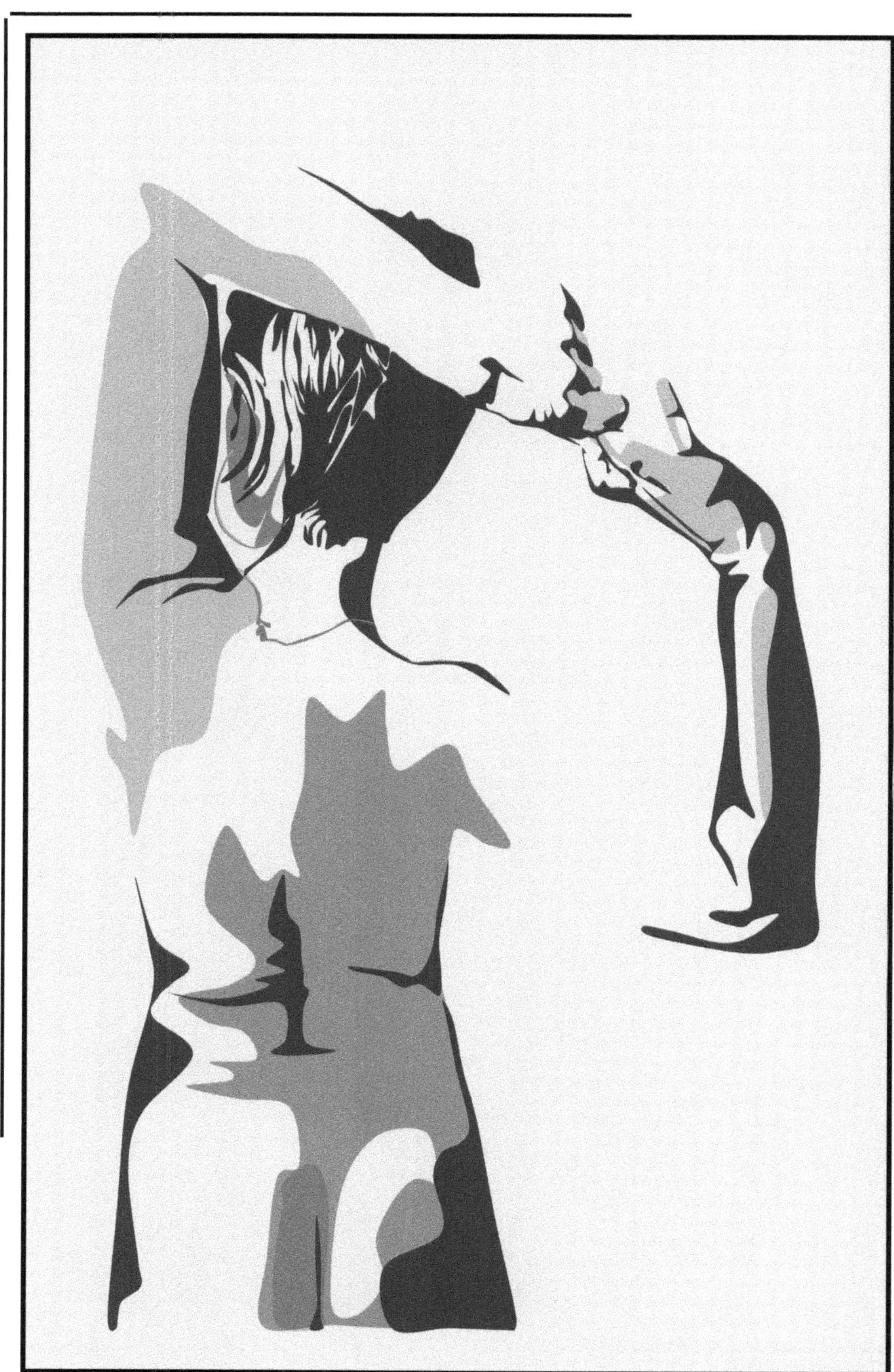

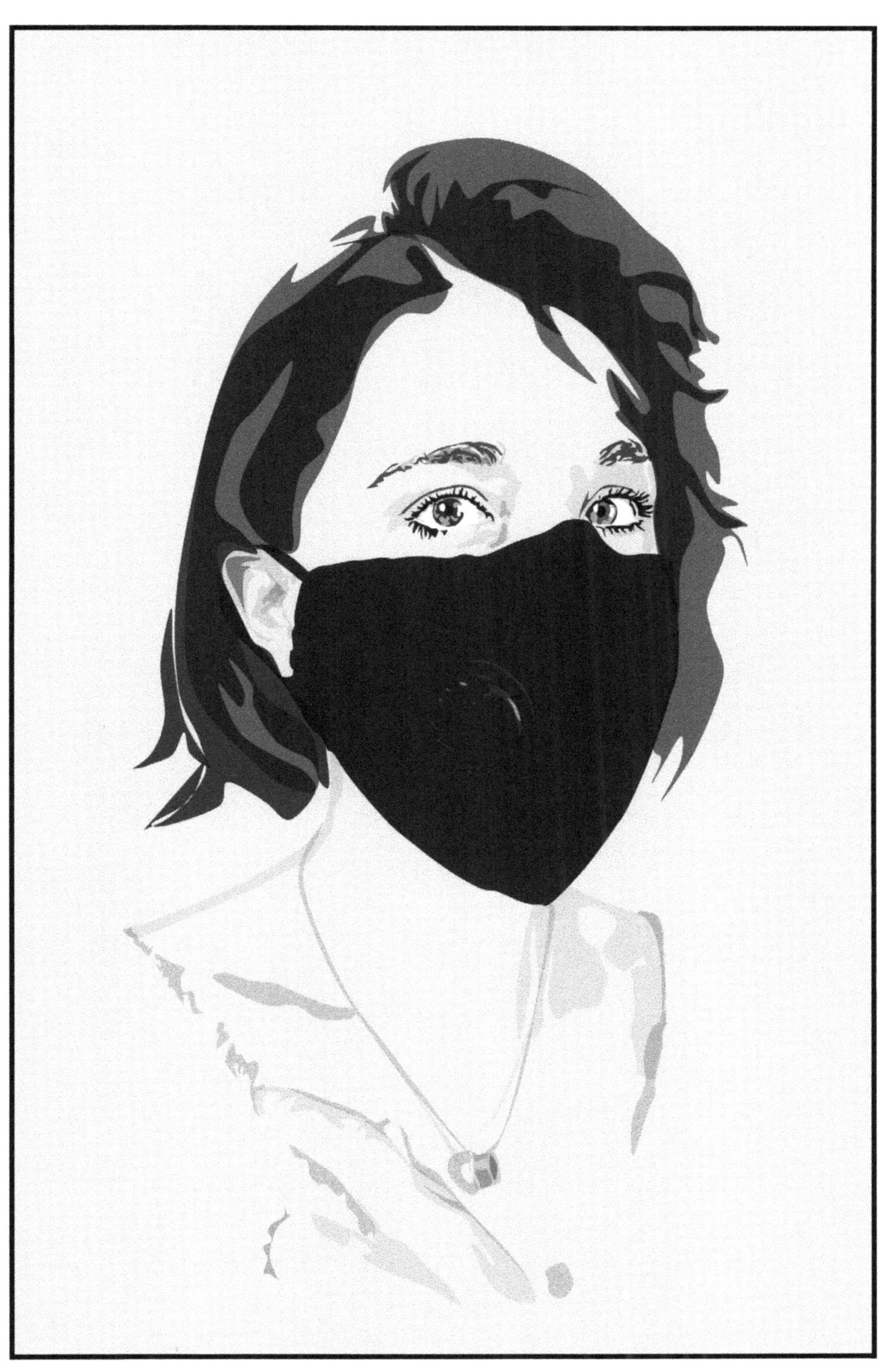

Body

Emily Benson

I wish I could dissect myself
Pull apart this body
Like a butcher
Excise the fat and gristle
Exhume the tumor
Scrape the cysts from my cervix
Lift my mind from my cranium
That cave of meat
Hone each limb
And dress it
Render the drippings
To coat the grating joints
Scrape the hair from the hide
Tone and sculpt
Find the old angles and
Make it all work right
Send the impulses to the nerves
Of pleasure instead of pain
I am weary of refusing
On the basis of this weak flesh
My spirit inextricably bound
To bold desire as a sense of self
Somehow I have become trapped
And if I could slip this
Noose of form
I'd find my way to you again

Letter to a Ghost

Brandyce Ingram

I remember when you became atoms

Sparsed into binary switches
On—off—black—white
That allowed space in your body
To breathe.

I remember when you found your shadow

Baked into the roasted grass
Like a deflated balloon—
"Shadows don't belong in the sunlight,"
I told you.

I remember when you visited me

Surprised to find your past
Could talk back to you—
As if I hadn't been calling all along
To your air.

I remember when you found your home

Dilapidated but still warm
Geometric—crumbling—sharp—still
You stand tall and sure,
Empty as pockets.

Chicago Quarantined

Michelle Geoga

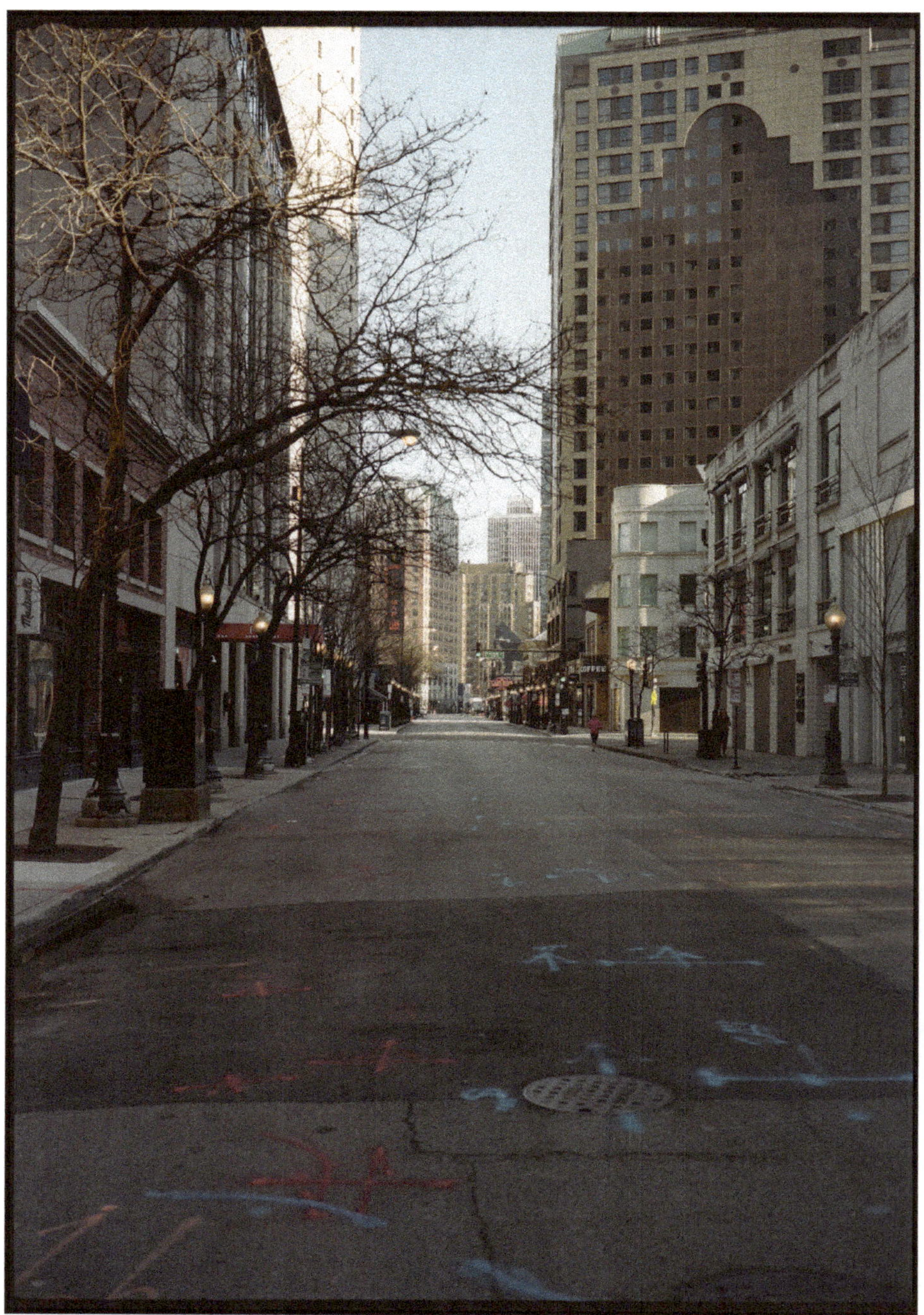

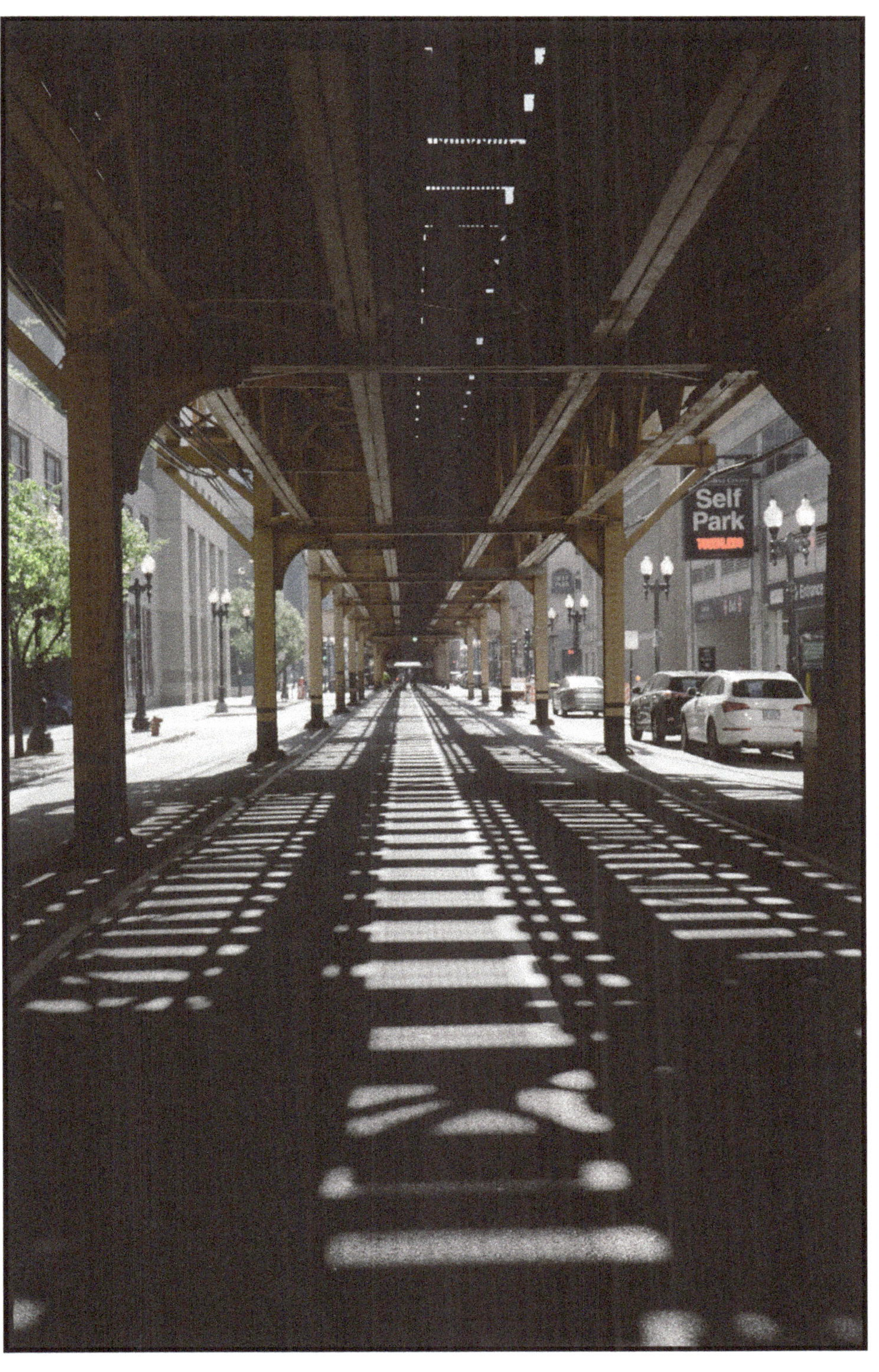

Self
Park

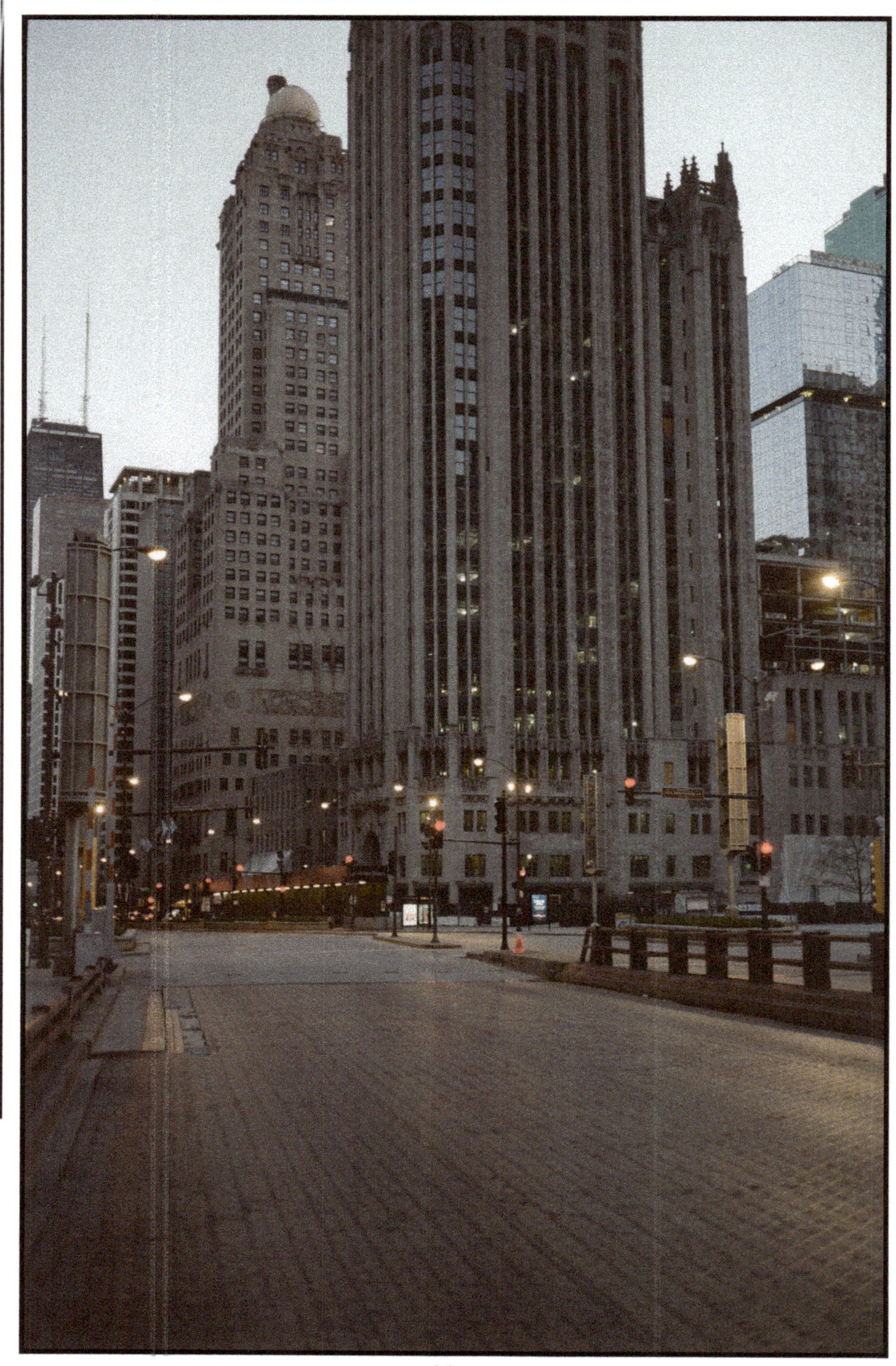

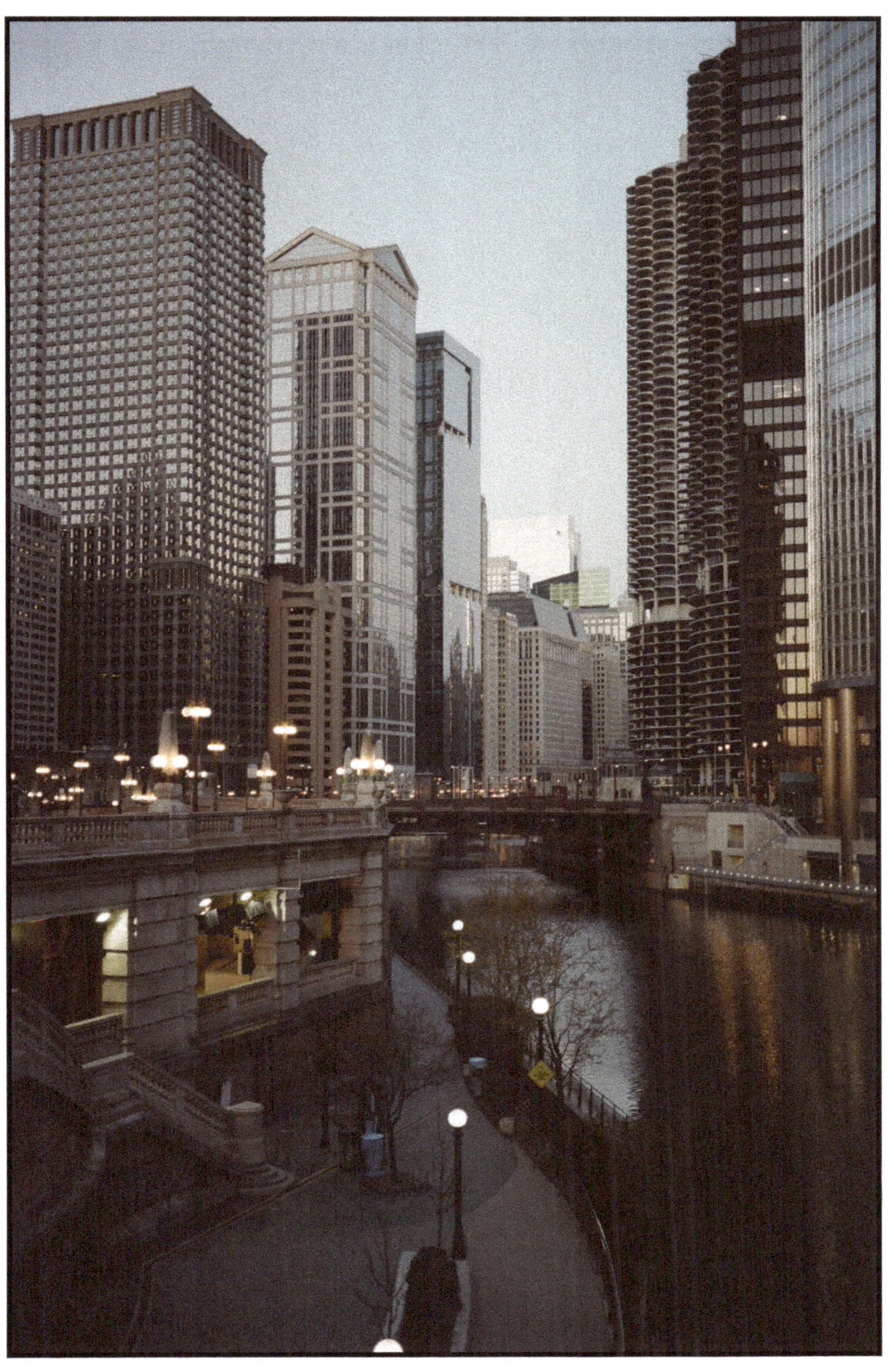

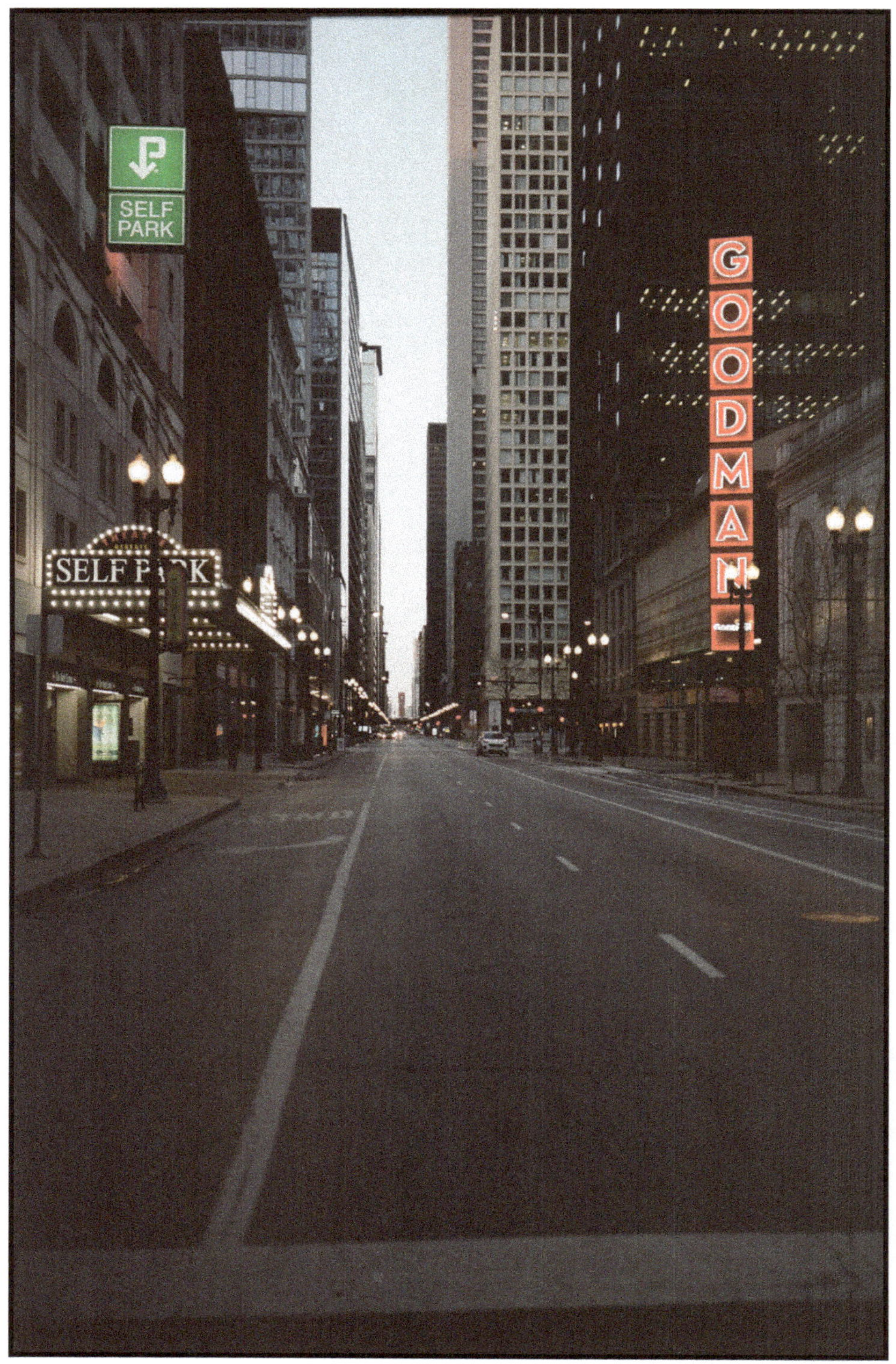

SELF
PARK
SELF PARK
GOODMAN

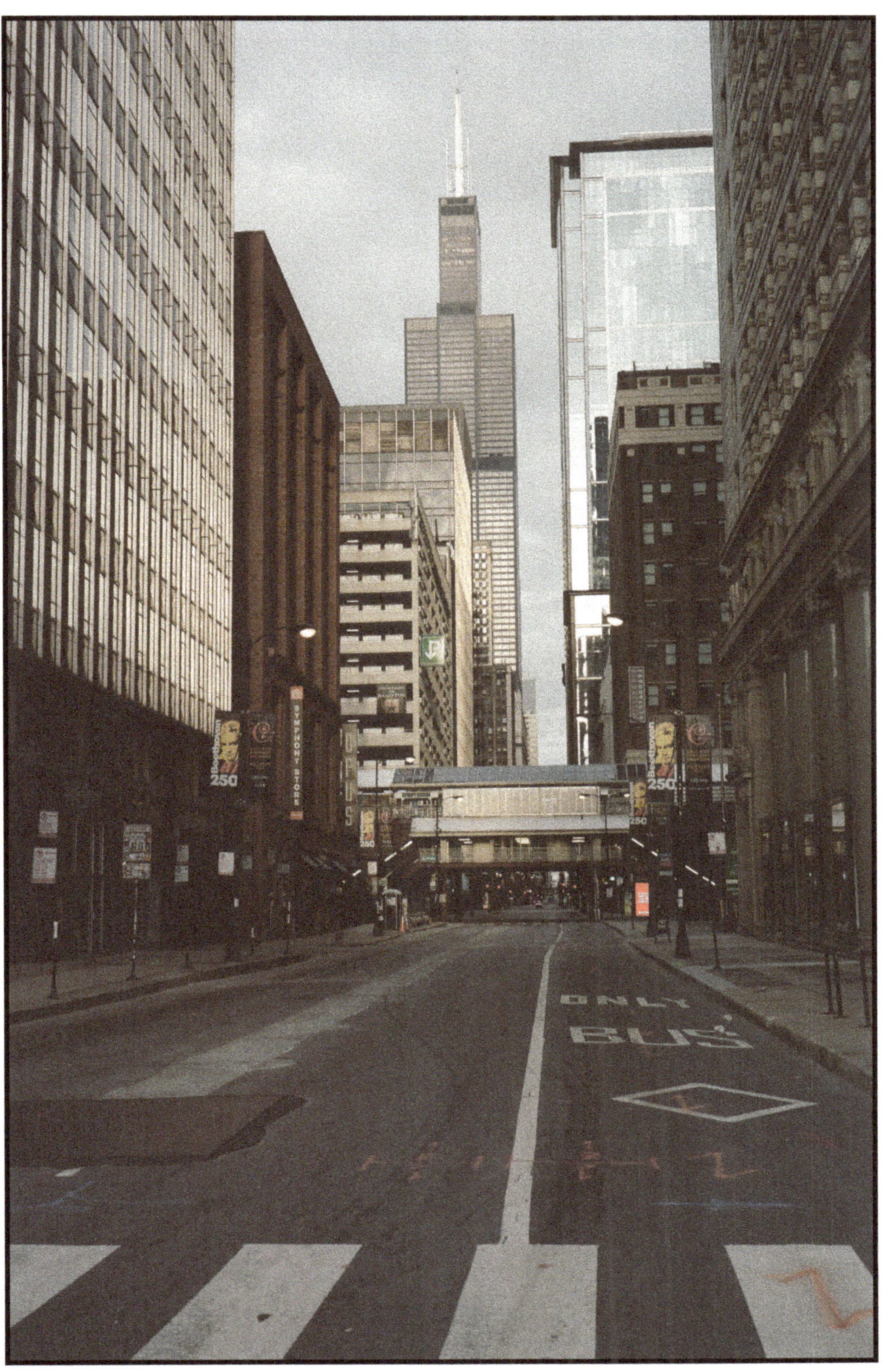

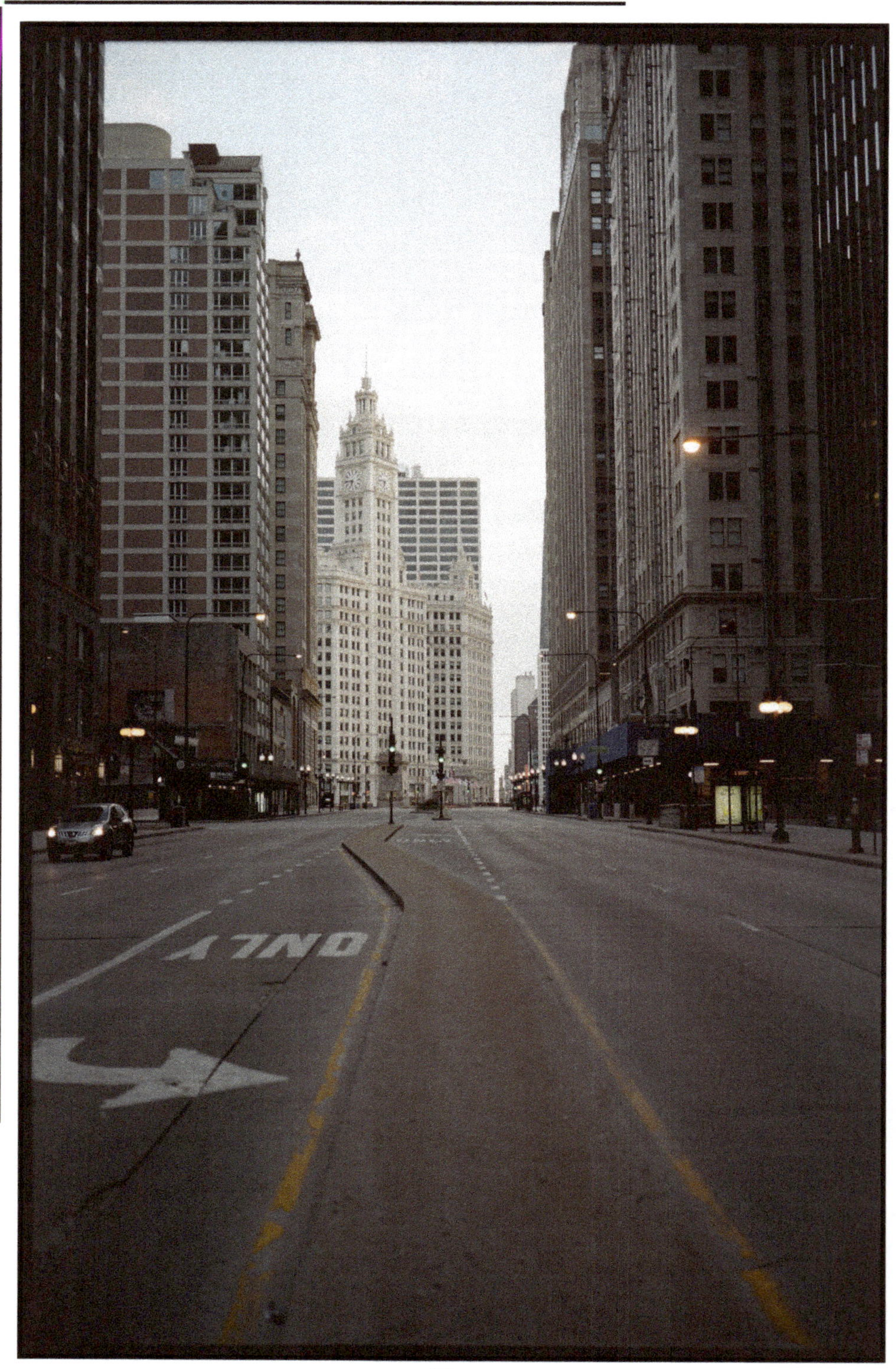

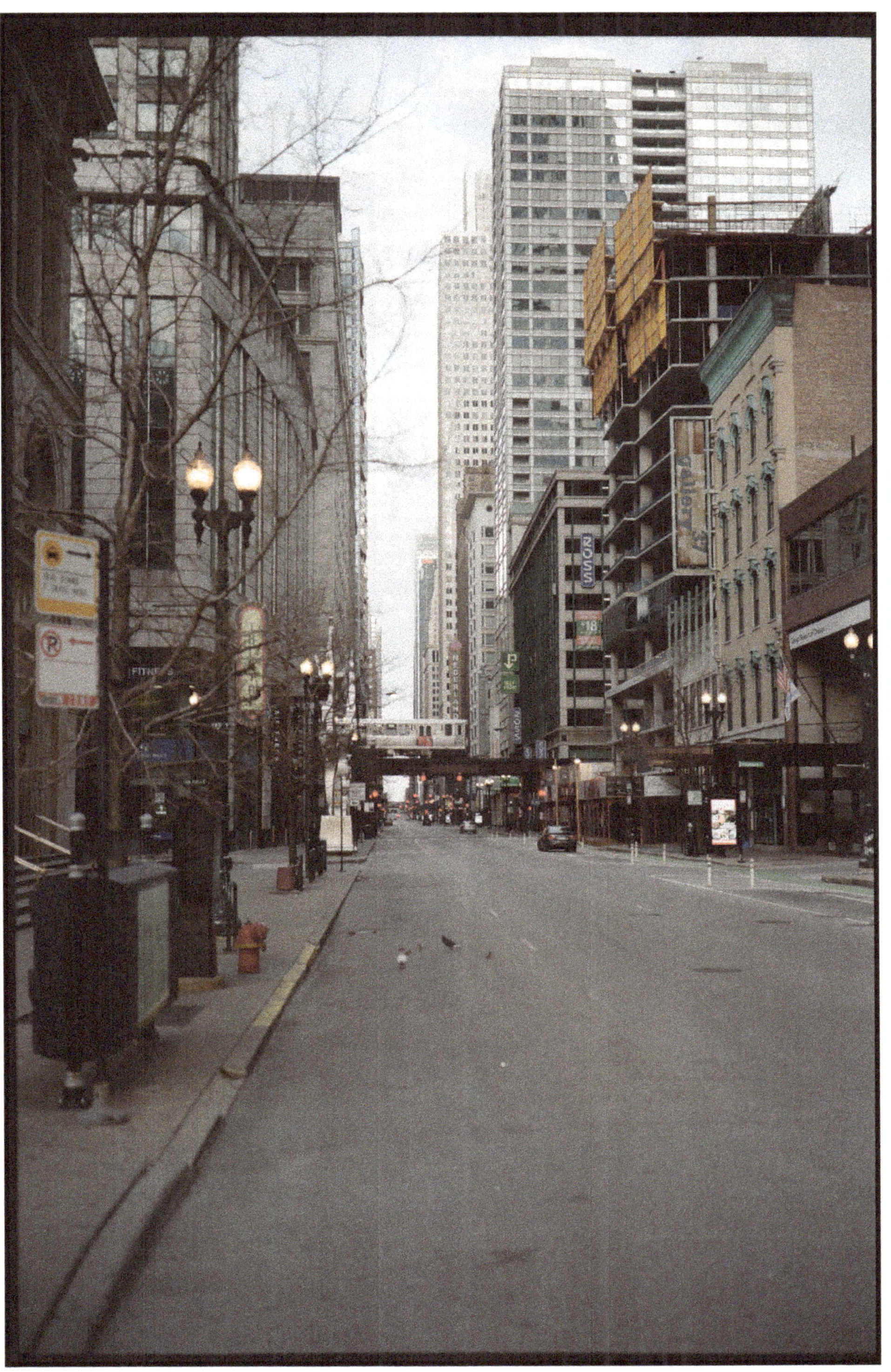

Why this is the best time to see your ex

Clara Mendoza

1. You cannot be overcome by leftover emotions and do something you will regret (six feet of distance is the perfect built-in barrier, and you can't even see their lips behind that piece of fabric)

2. You have gotten on that Youtube video workout kick and have never looked hotter, and don't you secretly want them to miss you (just a little bit)

3. No one's face really looks that great with a mask, so you won't even have to find them attractive (don't worry, you'll still look great to them, I promise)

4. When they tell a joke, you only have to crinkle your eyes to make them feel funny (even though we both know you were always the funny one)

5. They're probably so desperate for human contact that it makes you seem 8x hotter then you are (but you already know you're sooo out of their league)

6. The mask will hide your horror when they start discussing the new person they are talking to (just admit to yourself that you're not over them and go get some ice-cream)

7. You will have an excuse not to see them again when you end up catching feelings "my mom/grandmother/father/etc. is high risk" (the virus will keep getting bad again, after all)

8. You can justify your feelings to yourself by saying you just miss human contact (we both know thats not all it is sweetie, and that's okay)

Food Chain

Paul Ilechko

I lost the boat   that I was supposed to be
        traveling in   perhaps it flipped
            over   like a kayak

they told me   it was customized to meet
        my needs   sized and shaped
        with pulsating commerce

scraped and spooned   from the wet-ink
        darkness of its beginnings

beneath it   a floating equilibrium
        of aquatic depth   above it
            a million birds

in every possible color   crossing
        the globe   along static arcs that map
            to interstitial territories

*   *   *   *   *   *   *   *   *

Disease spreads along the same pathways
as fish and fowl are integrated along a global
supply chain   the fields of sickness patterned
like the shadows cast by nomadic clouds

*   *   *   *   *   *   *   *   *

The radius of a circle   metaphorically
        attached to an arc   that swerves
            and scrapes through fields

and markets   an agriculture
        and an industry   that interweave
            themselves

there was meant to be language   and mystery
        and a hauntingly beautiful melody
            and this was to be our life

but the fleet sank   and the fields turned

chemical brown   and the birds
        plummeted from the skies

and our skins peeled   and we found ourselves
        stranded   with no way to escape

from this rocky beach   that erodes a little more
        each day   with the rising tide.

No Sanctuary.

Ciarán Ó Gríofa

*O'Brien's party... came to Tulach na hEaspog, blessed by bell, Mass and gold enshrined relics...In the sanctuary of this great church they remained that night, while their sentries guarded the approaches at the fords and vulnerable places.**

I

Perched on an ivied bridge, chewing grass,

 I shock you with a shove into space,

Catching you just in time: spliced laughter.

Watching the cattle all-the-day-down

Moving, as they graze, across the corcass,

the rumble as the bulk milk lorry passes,

throwing dust into the air about us.

II

Words are our touchstones, our relics.

 In the still evening, the black phone rings,

As the sun fades, between the tight houses,

the men with dogs are distant ghostly things,

while in the magnolia room, the unsaid pledge

 is cherished; yet this is a vulnerable place

 where the other voice is vital.

III

No church-shelter for us, burdened one,

We are more the sentinels at the ford,

unsure of our own footing, march-weary,

hoping our words will somehow see us through,

while we ache towards dawn and day talking

Where the dew rises from the empty corcass

Quenching fairy fires, spawning changelings.

**Quotation from "Wars of Torlough More O'Brien" by Sean Mac Ruairí Mac Craith 1459, translated by Standish Hayes O'Grady Irish Texts Society and also Sean P Ó Cillín in Ó Cillín , Sean P (Ed) Travellers in Clare 1459-1843 Galway, 1977.*

**This poem first appeared in Passengers Journal.*

Dialogue

Turner Hilliker

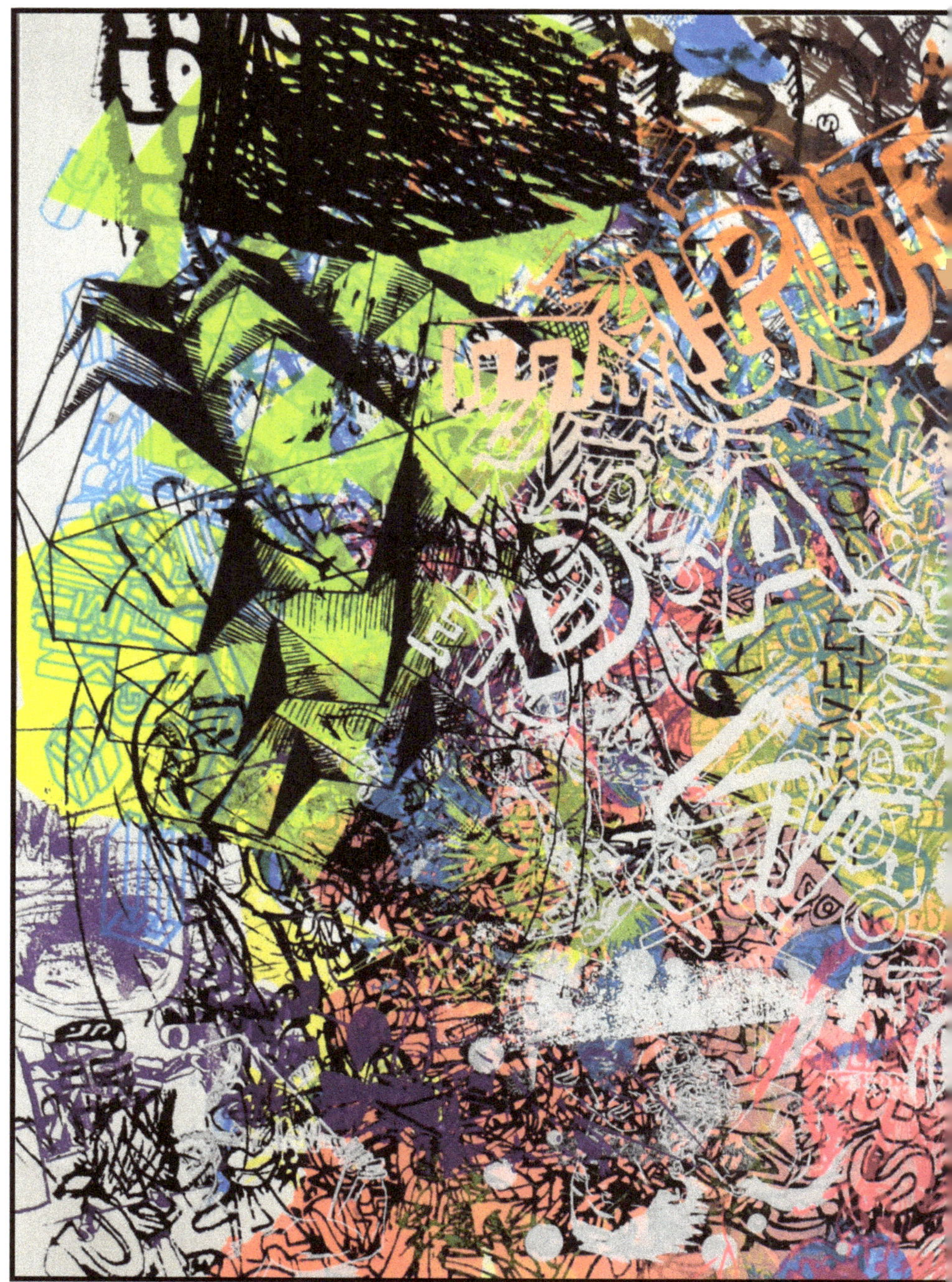

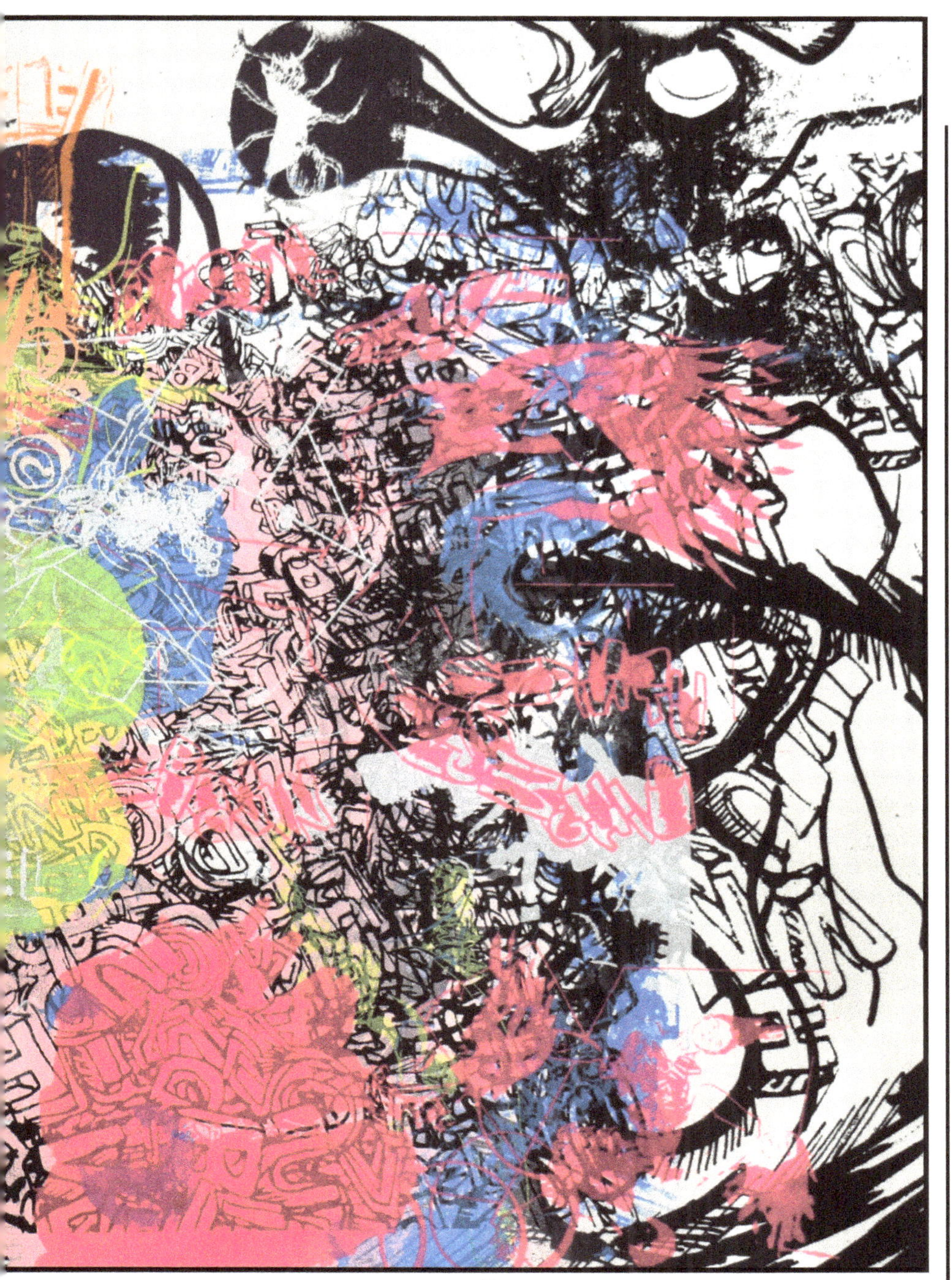

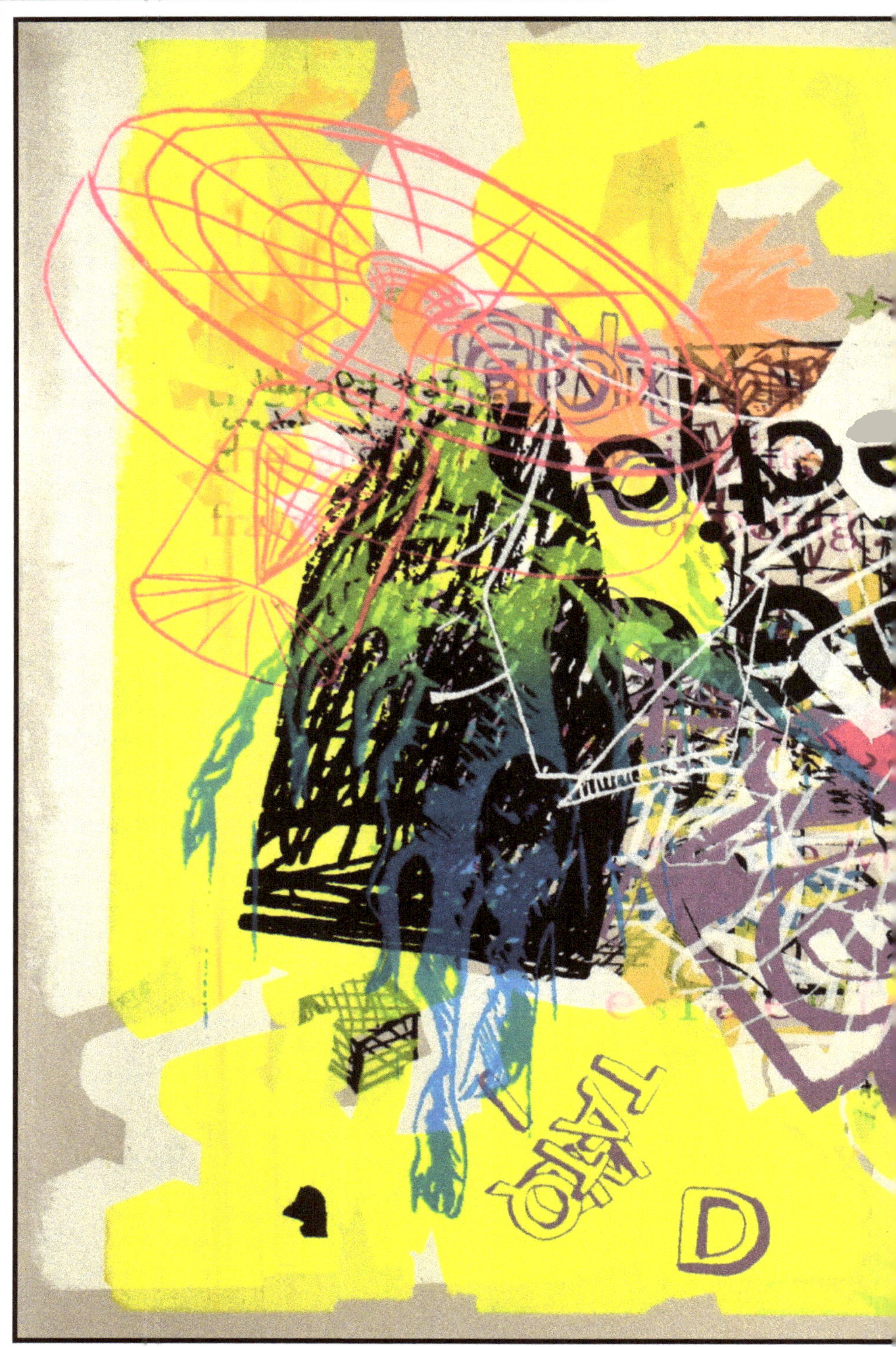

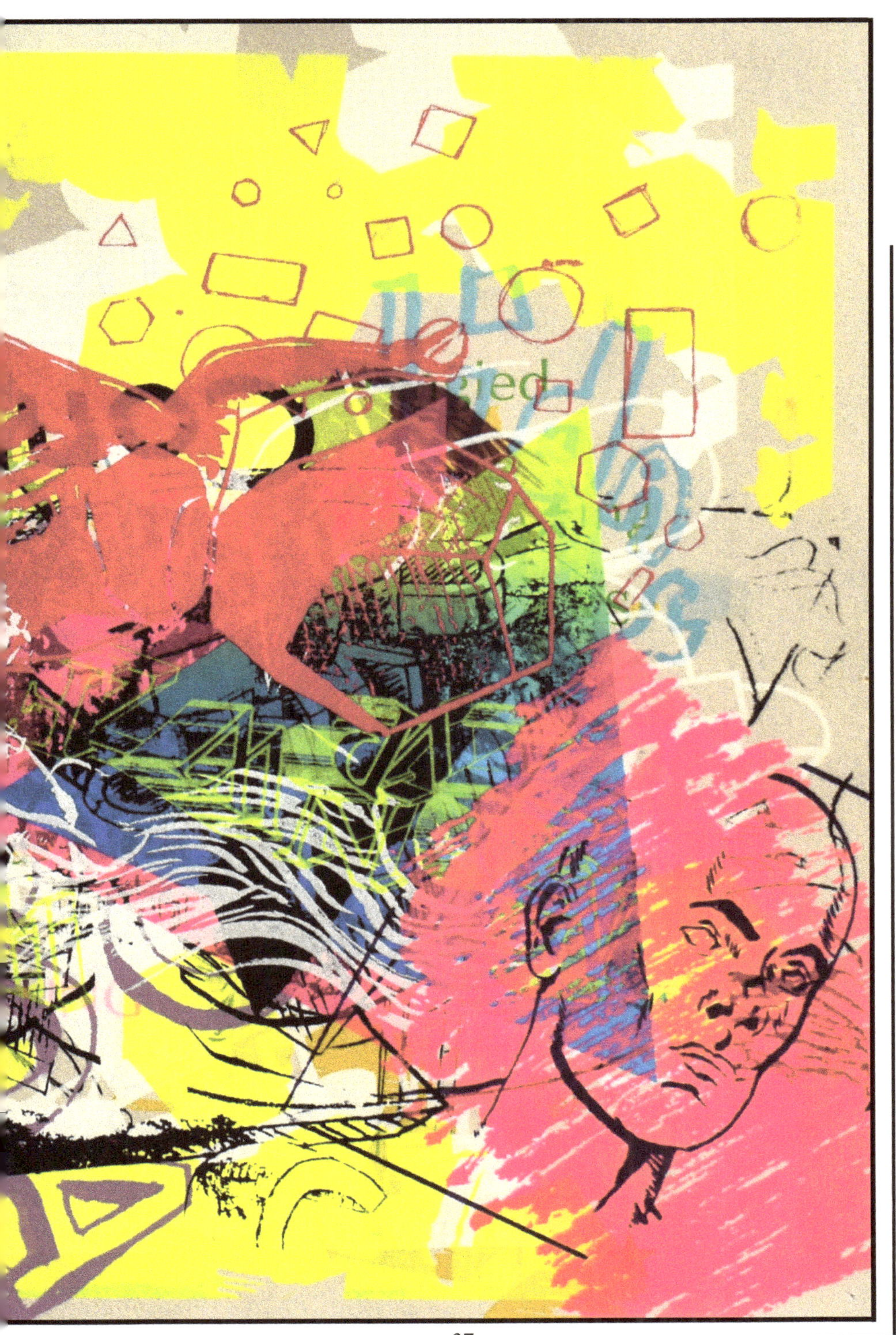

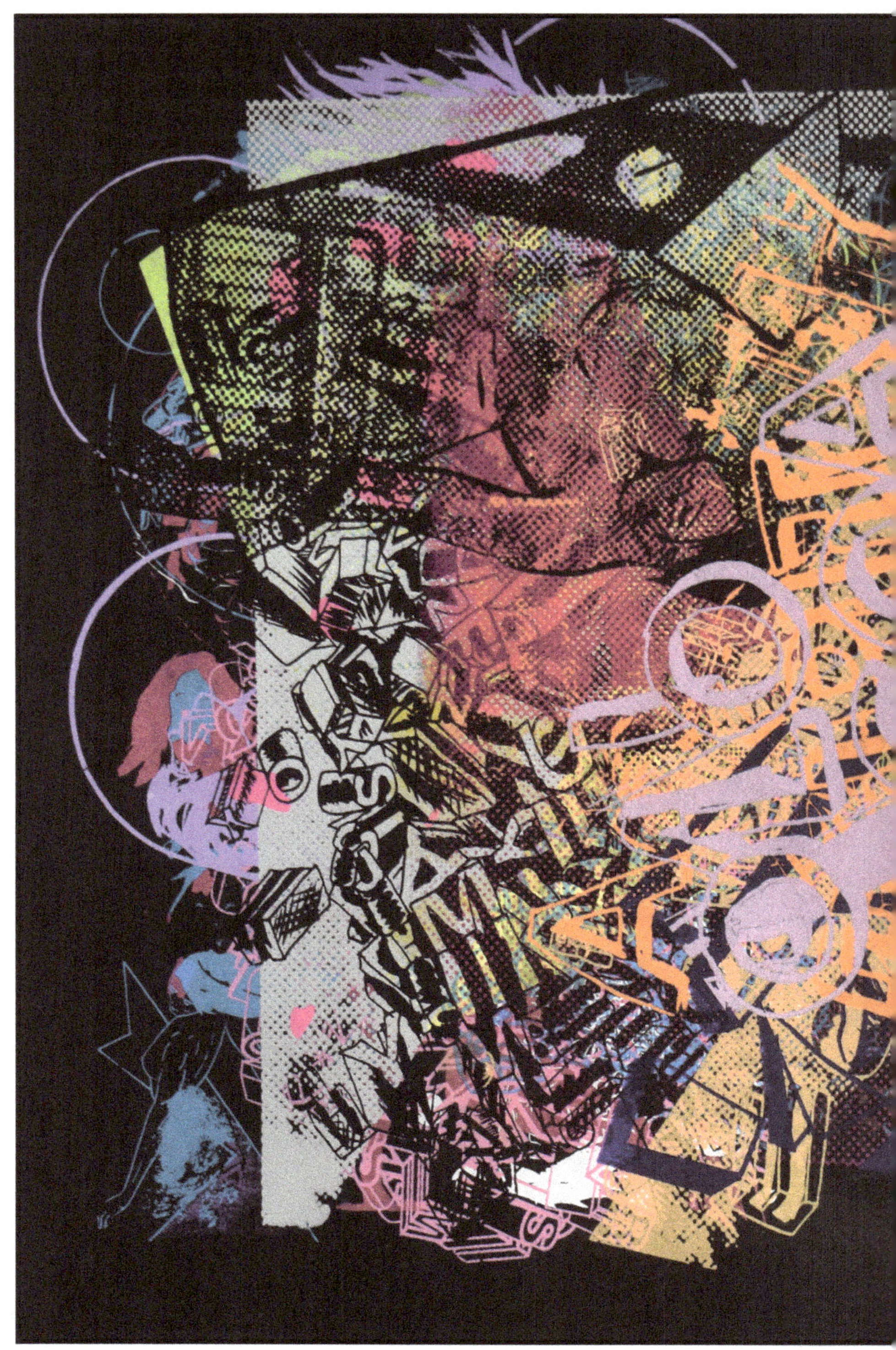

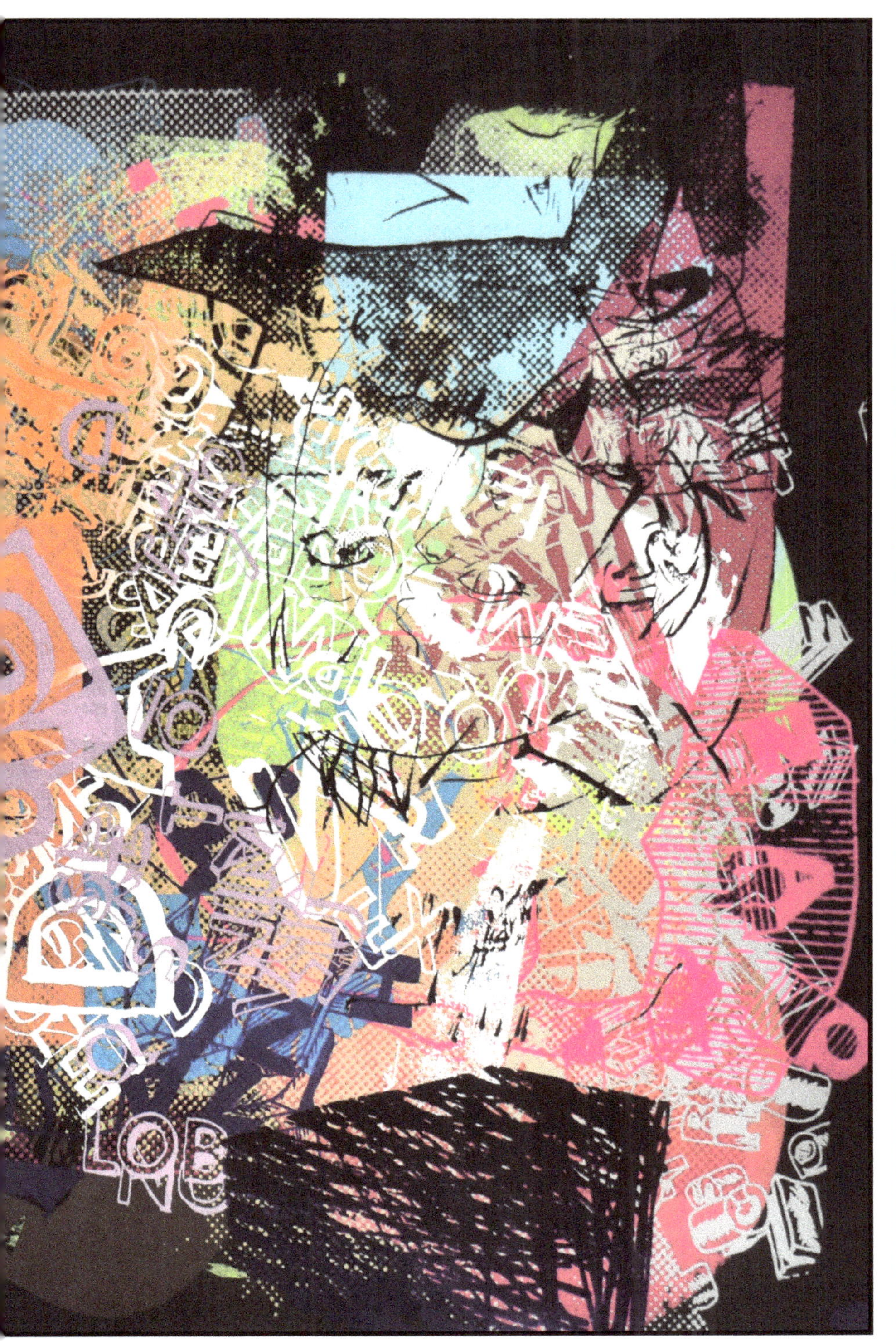

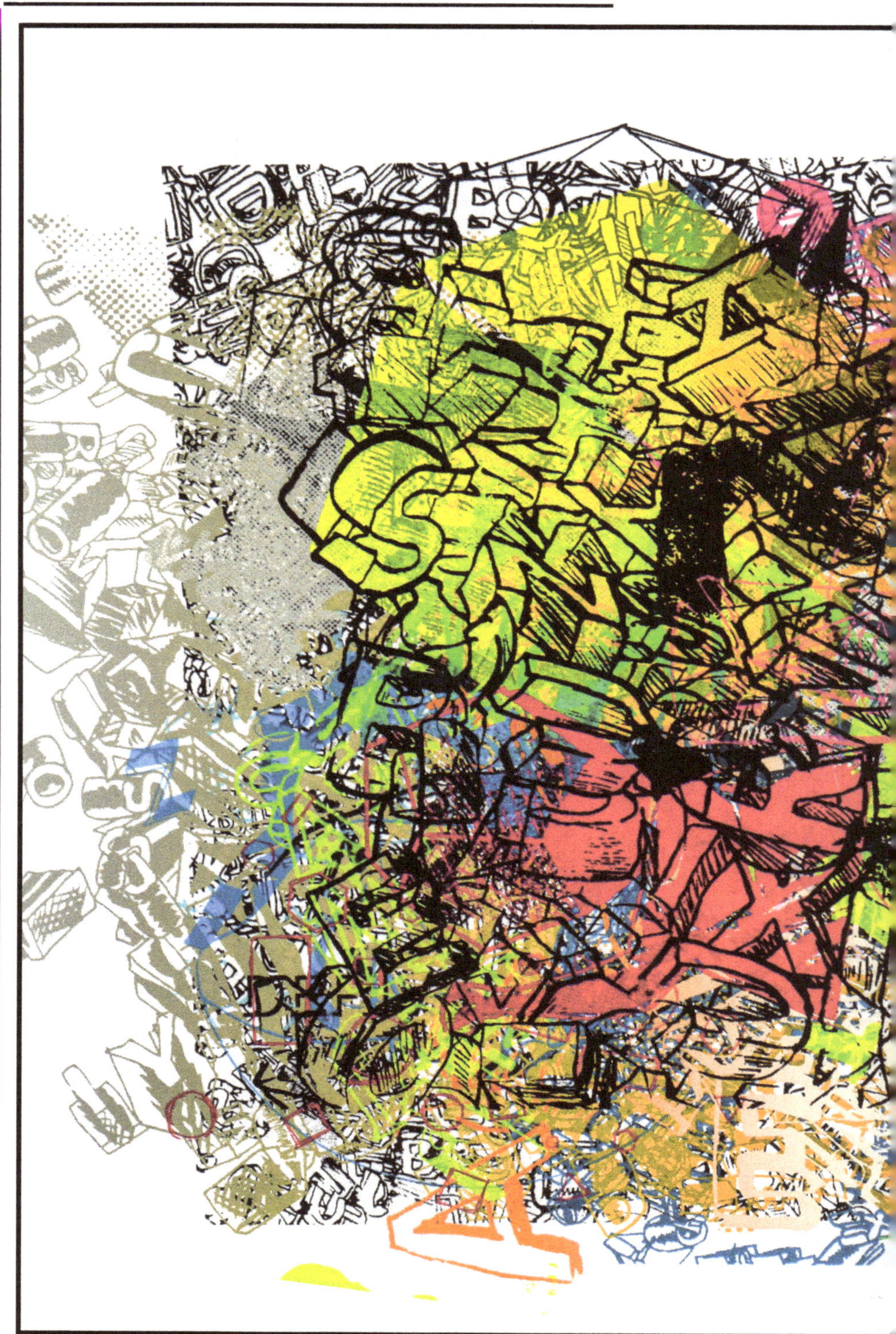

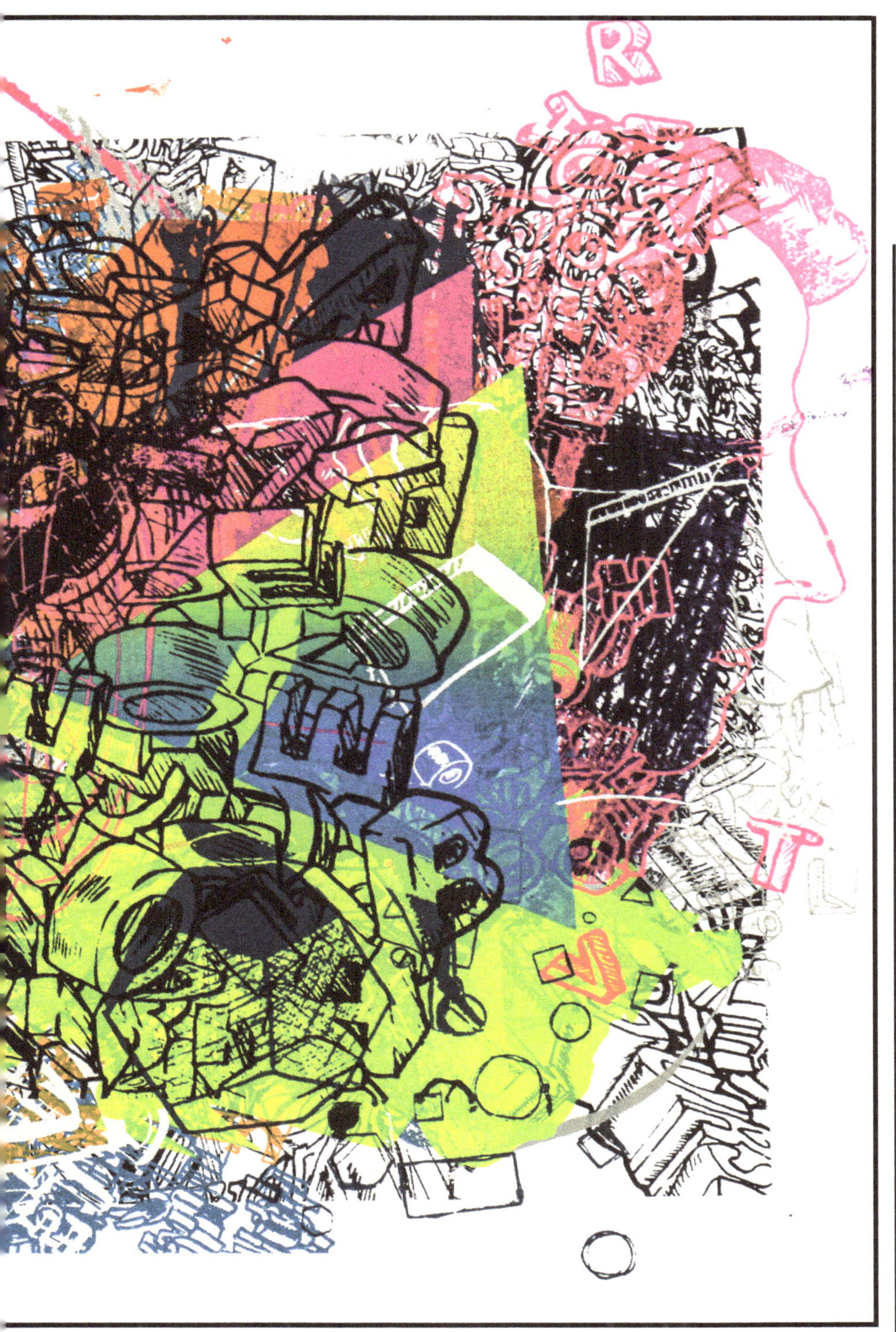

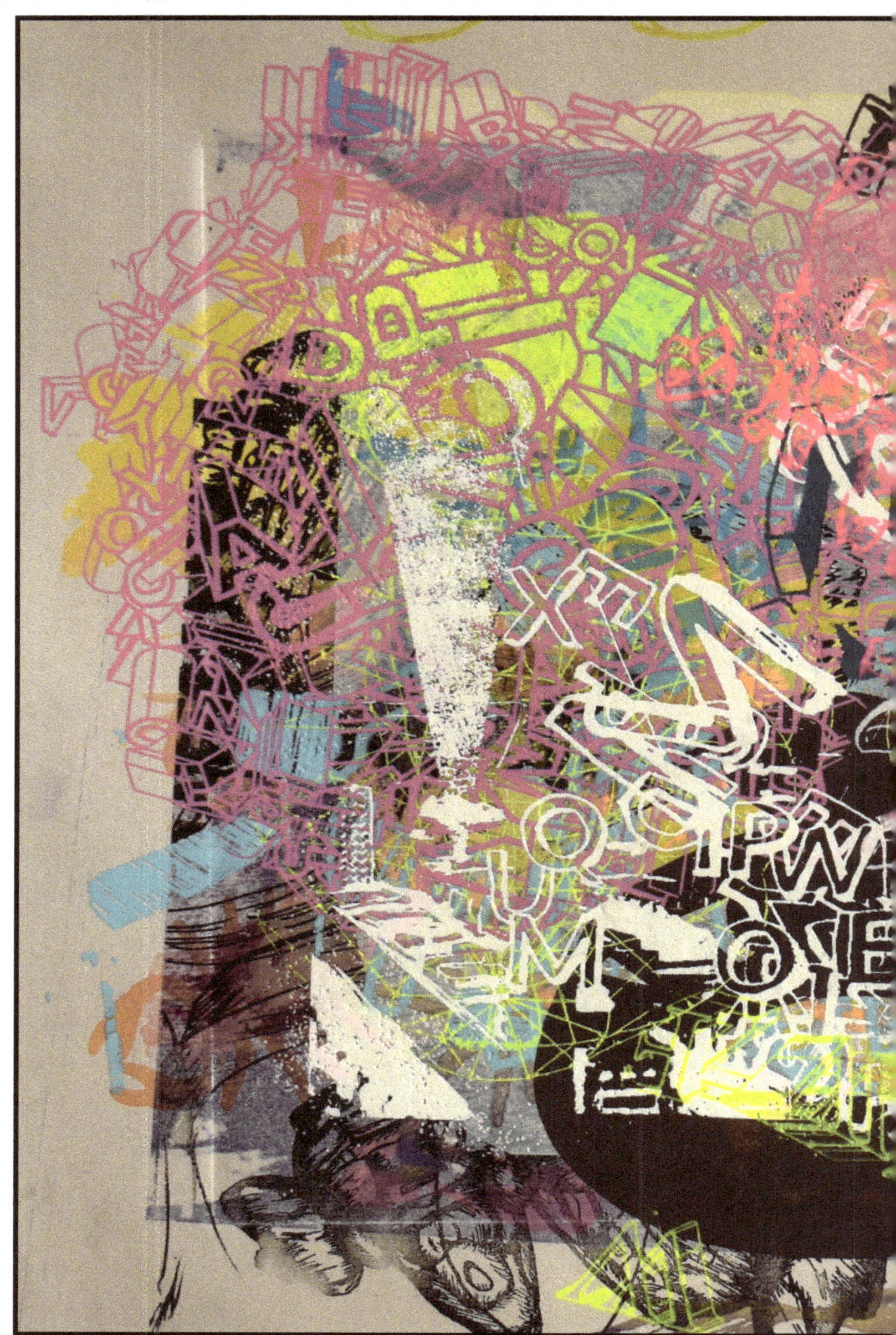

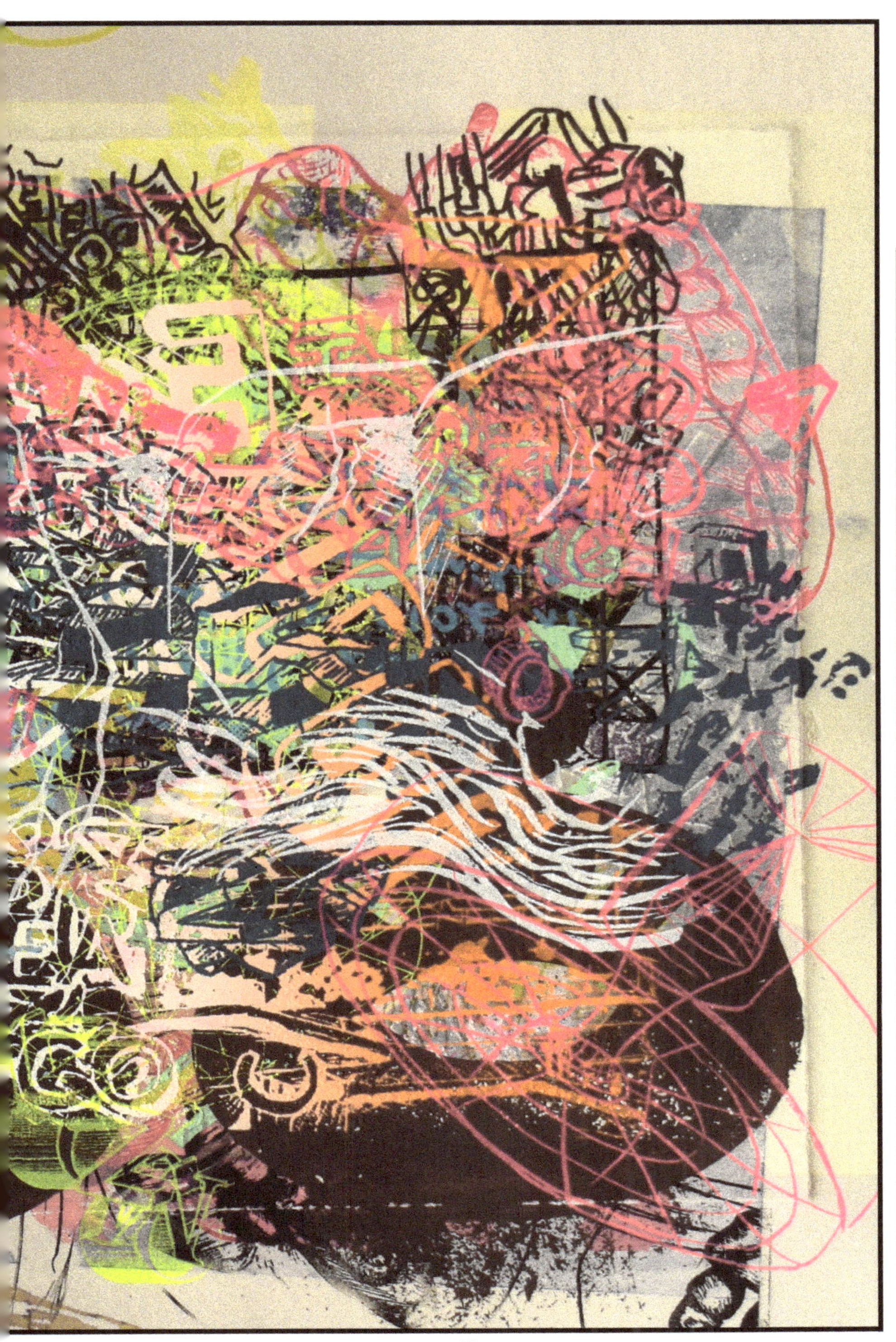

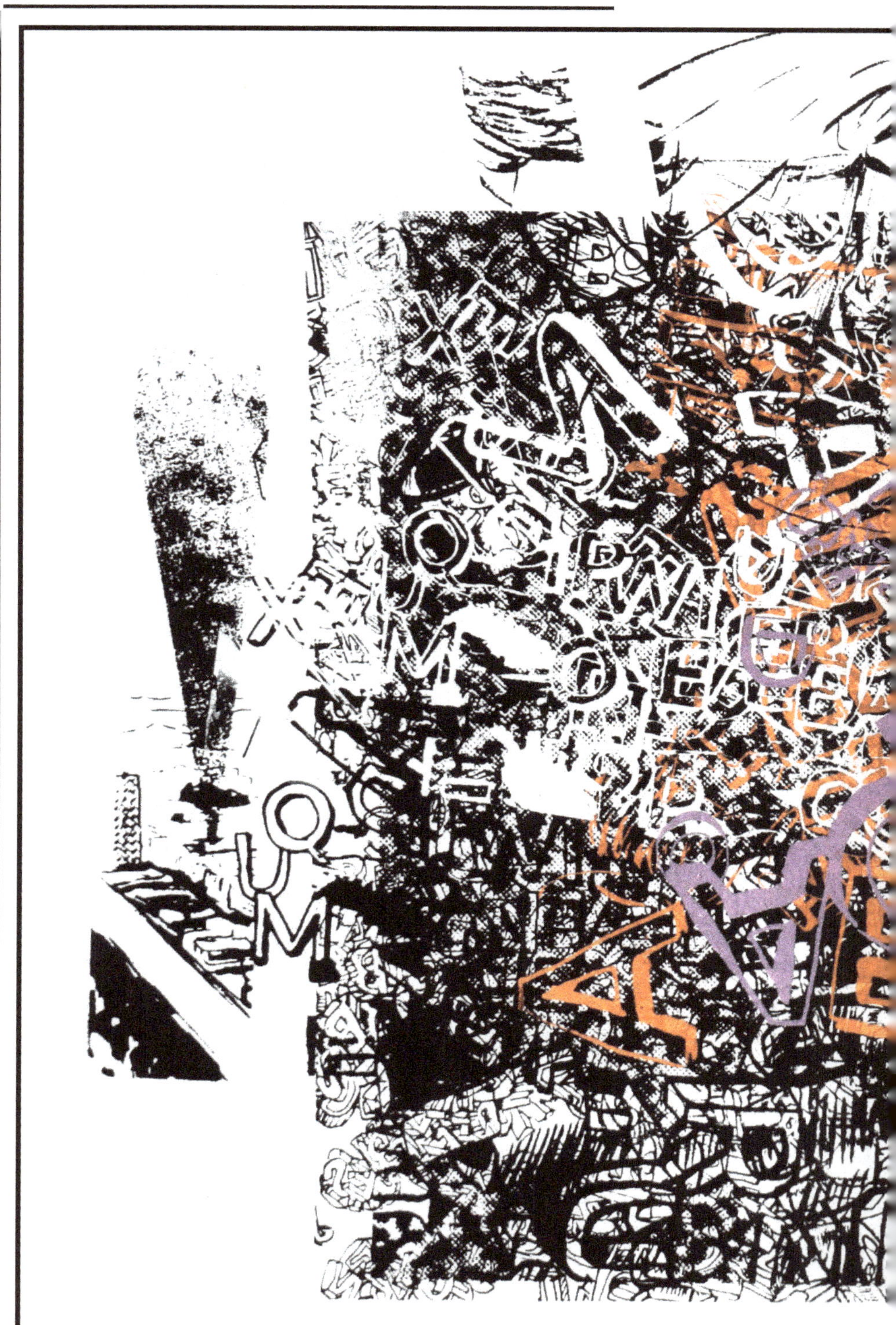

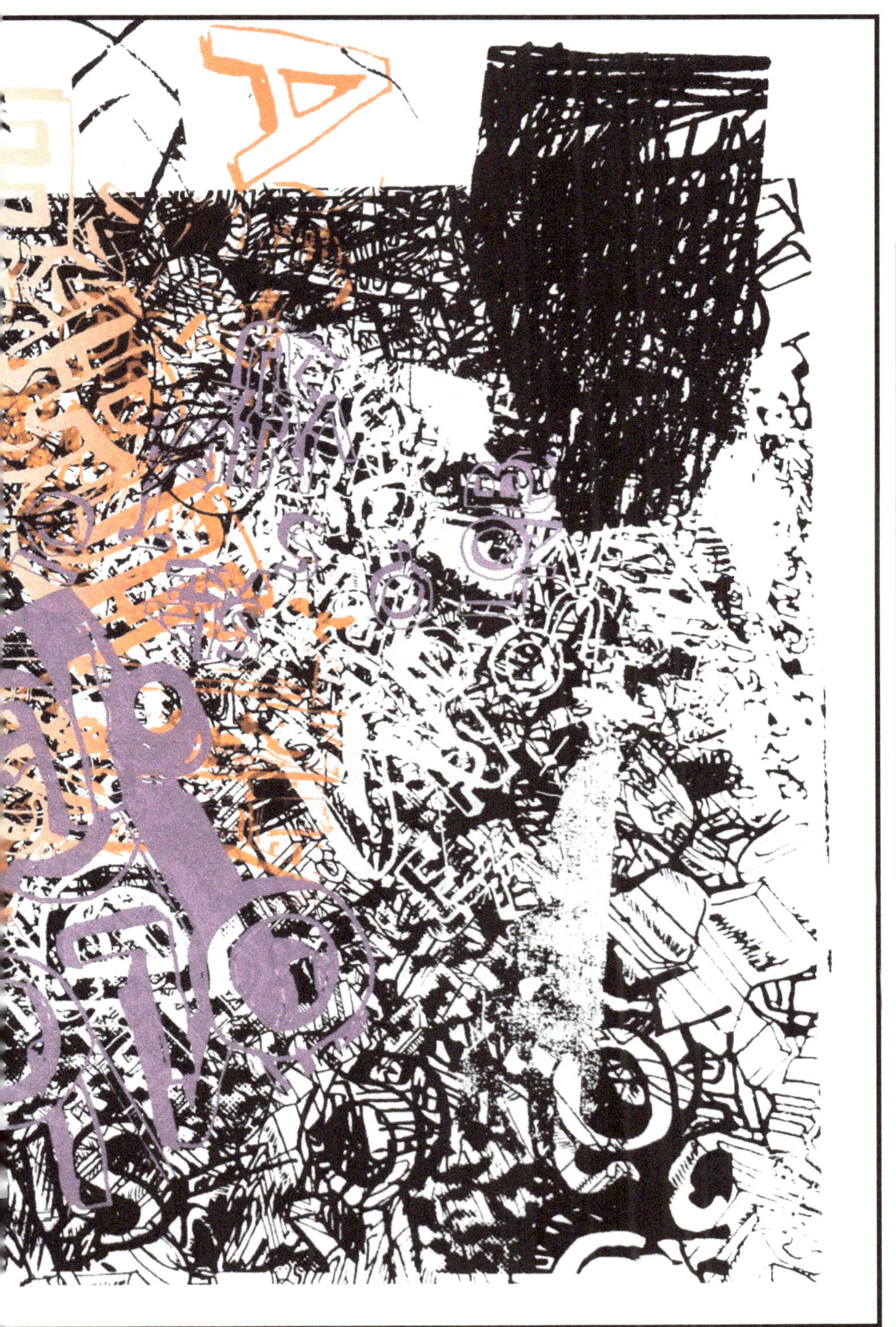

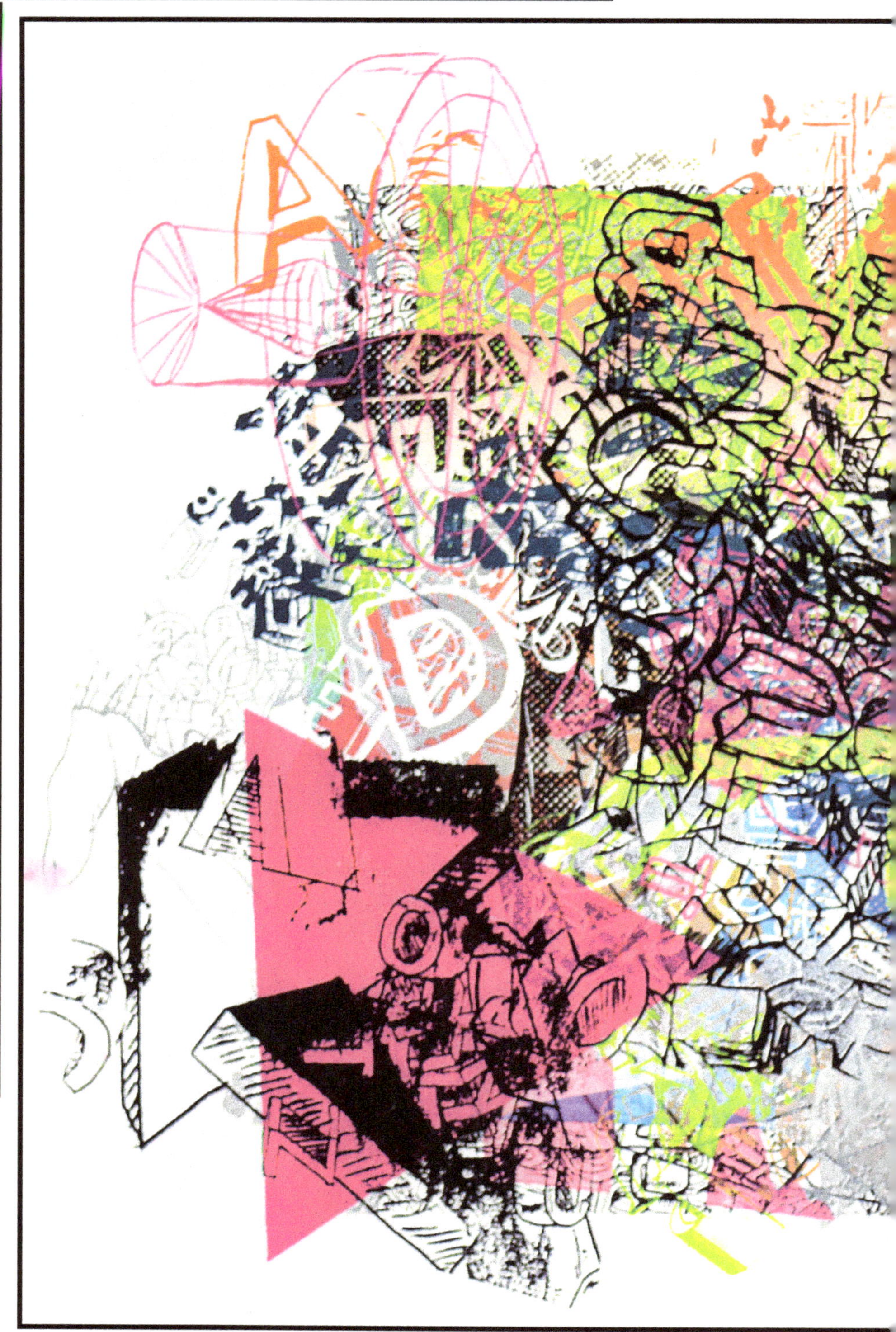

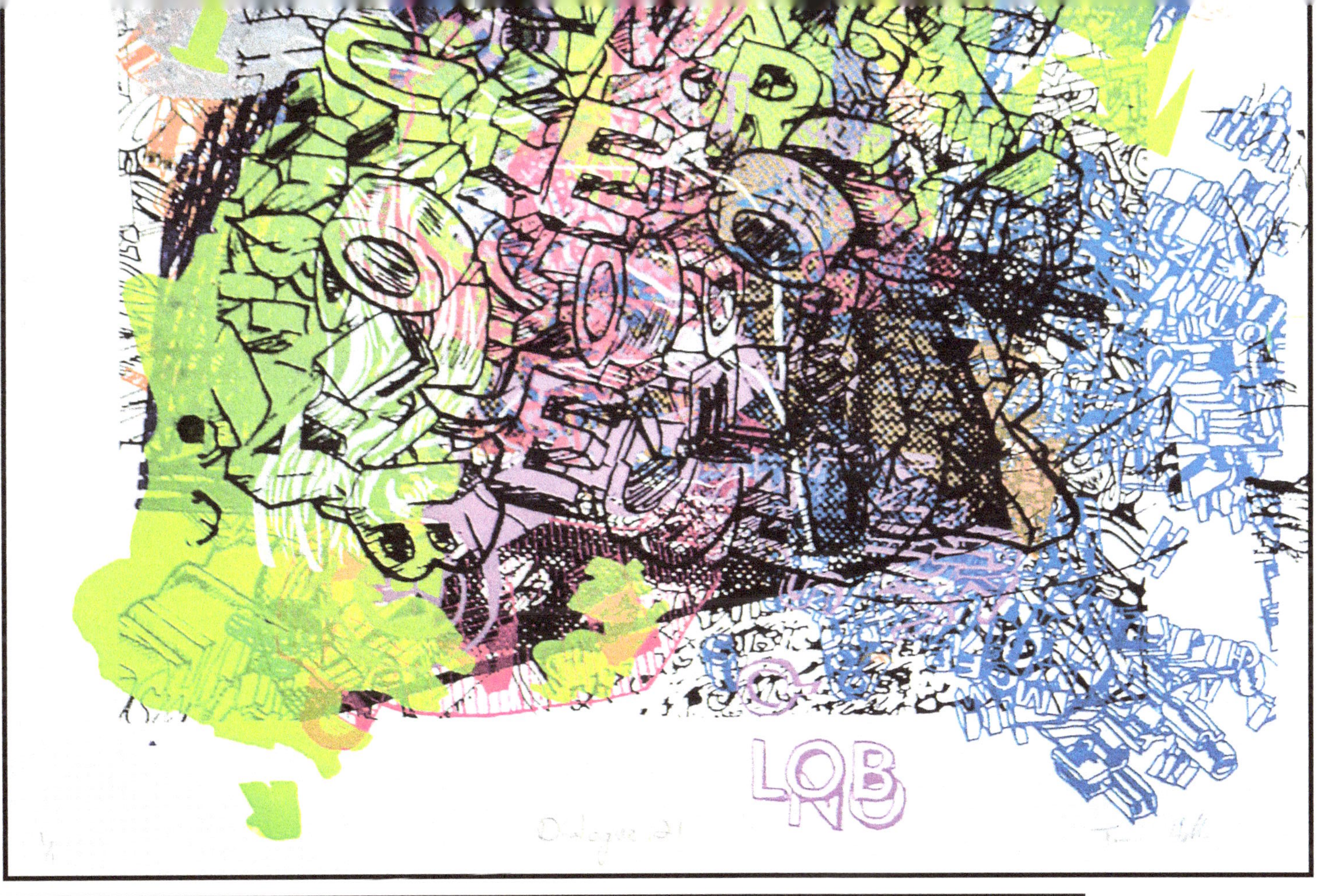

Anthropocene Fire Gardens

Ann-Marie Brown

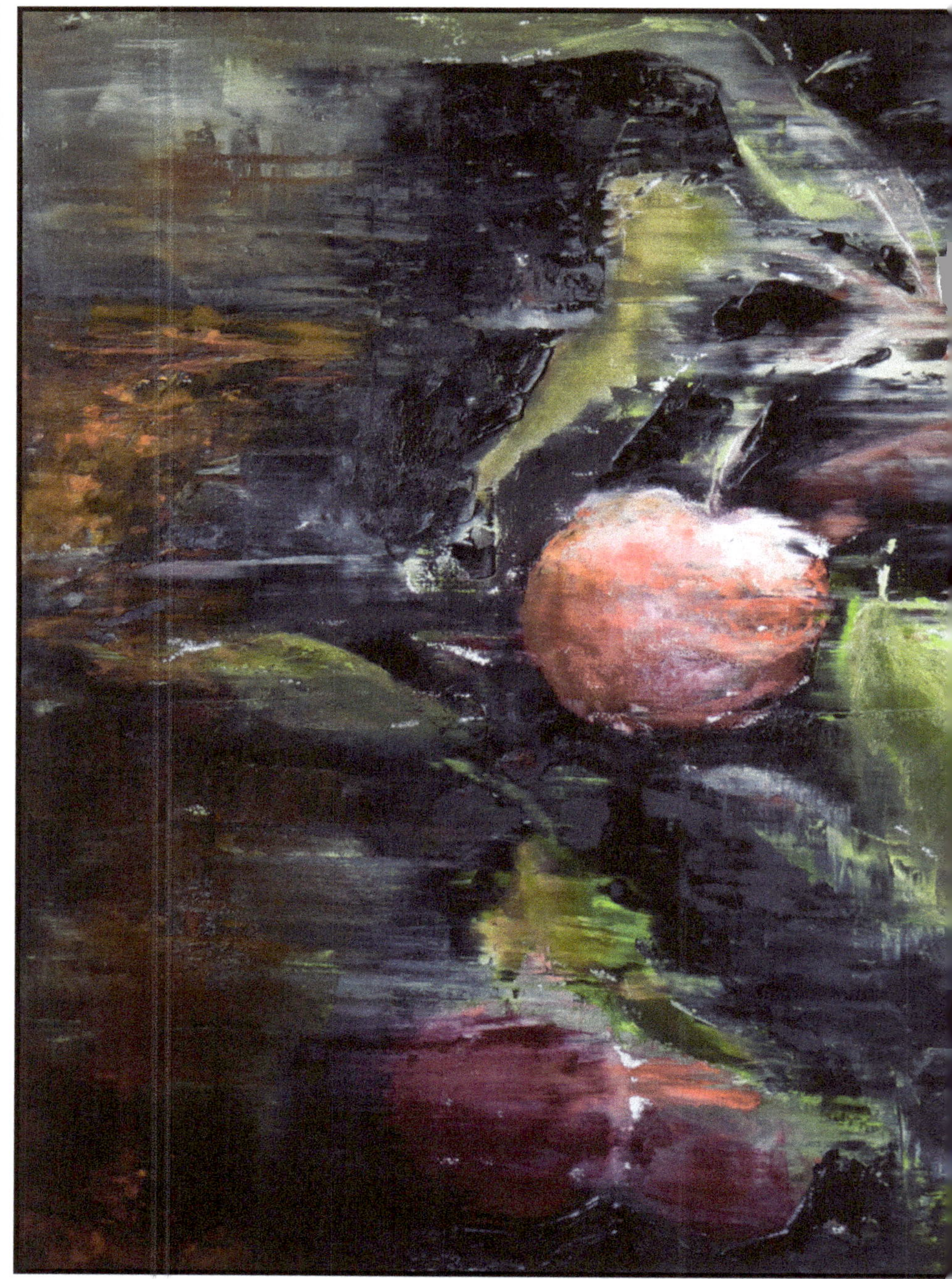

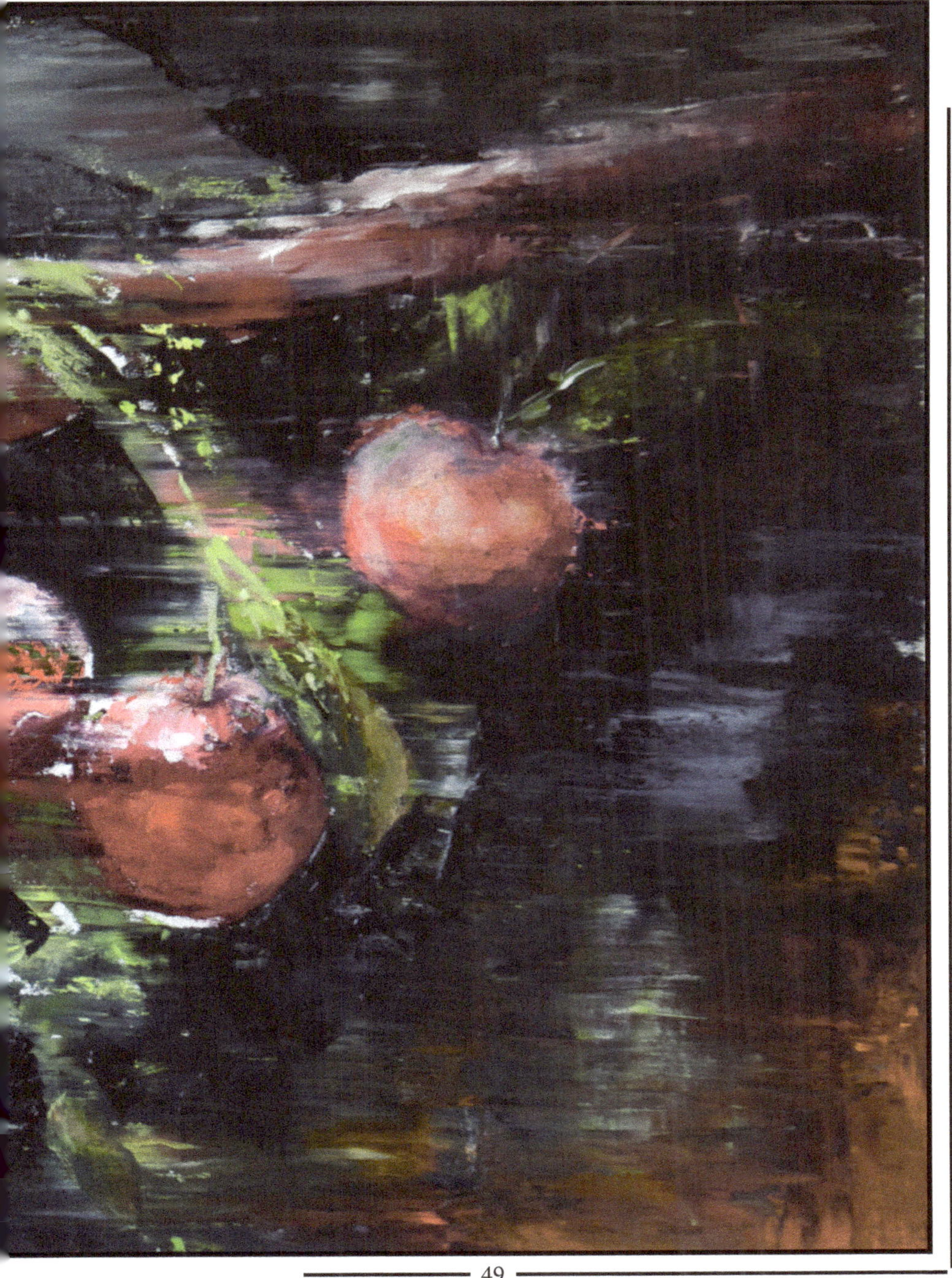

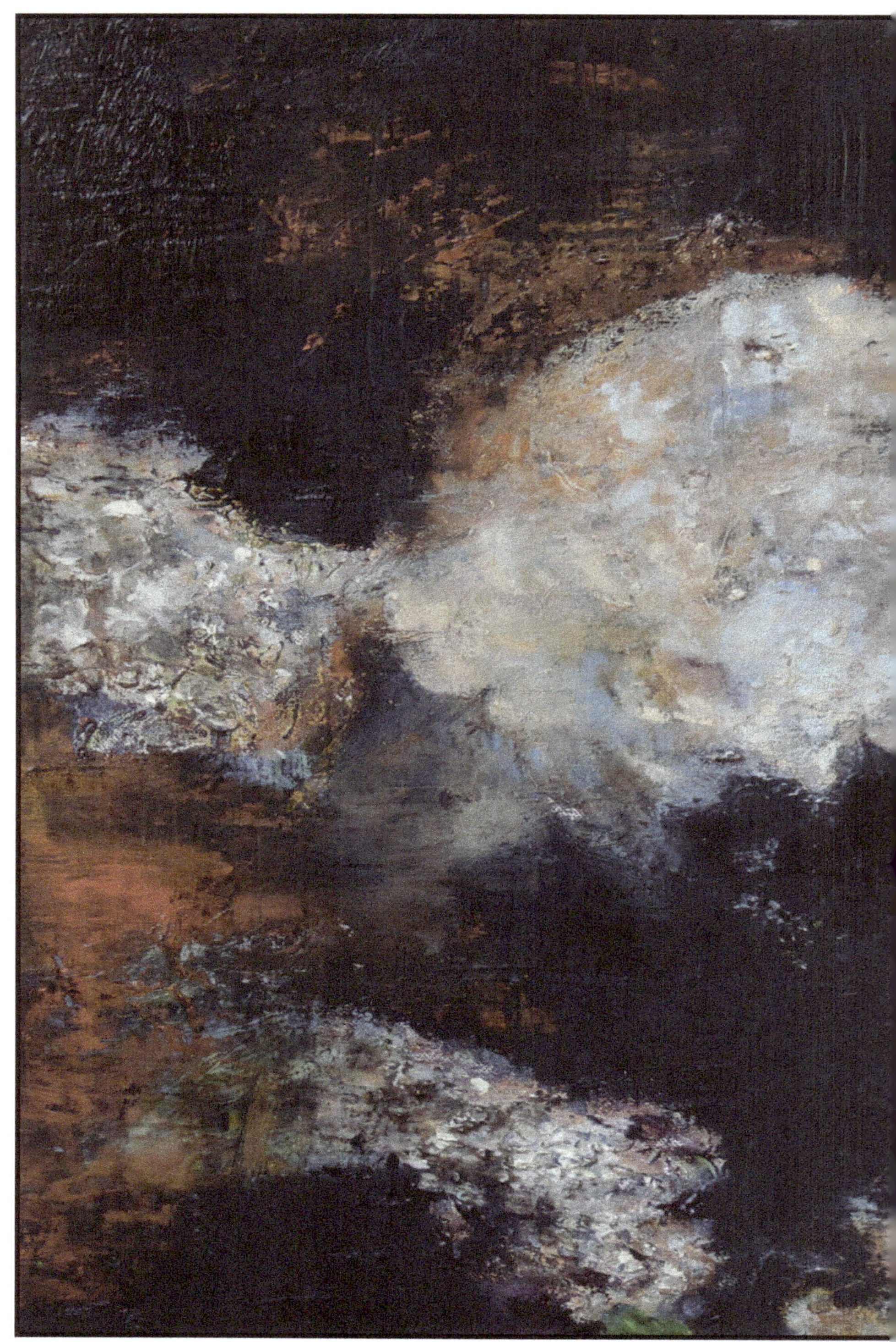

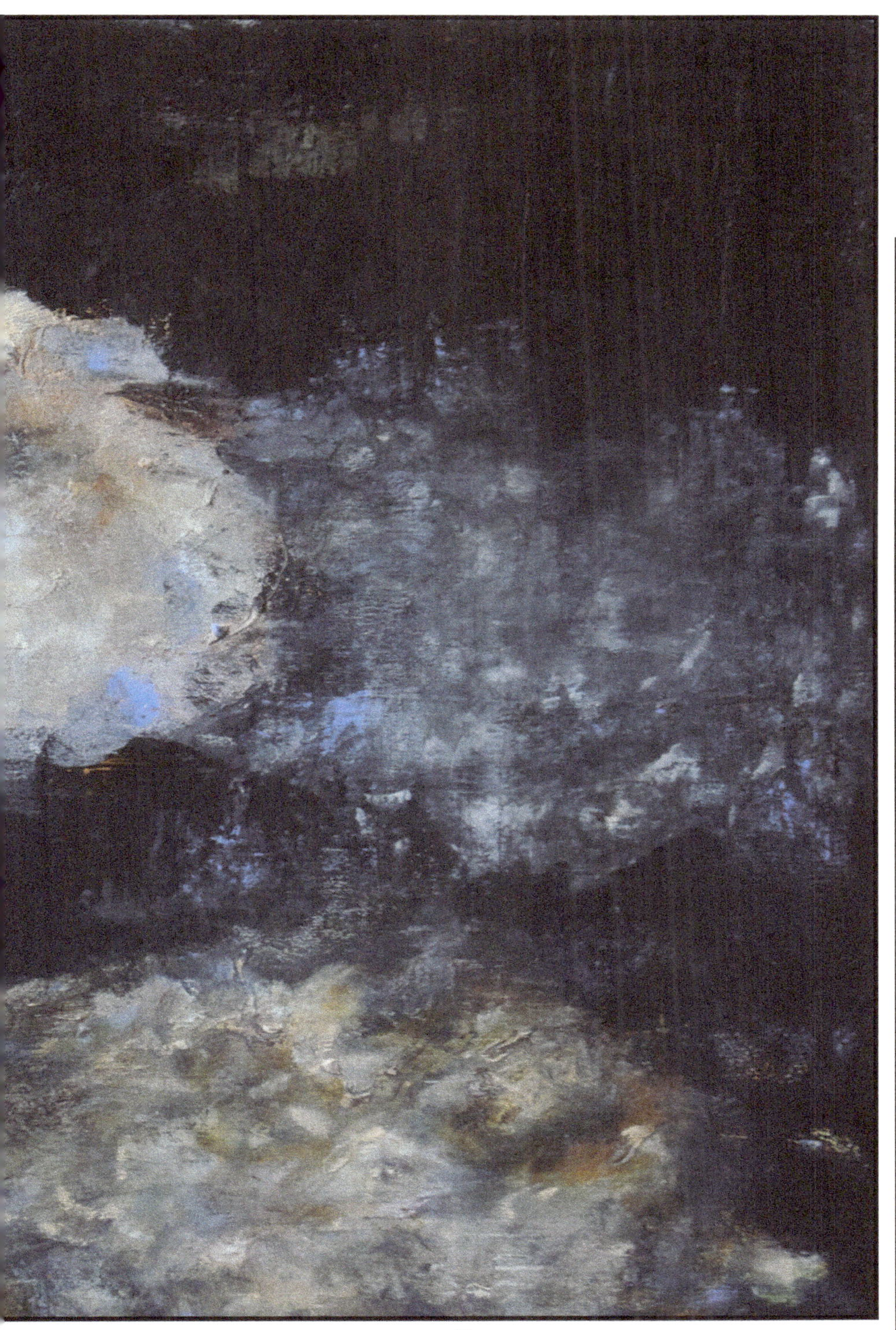

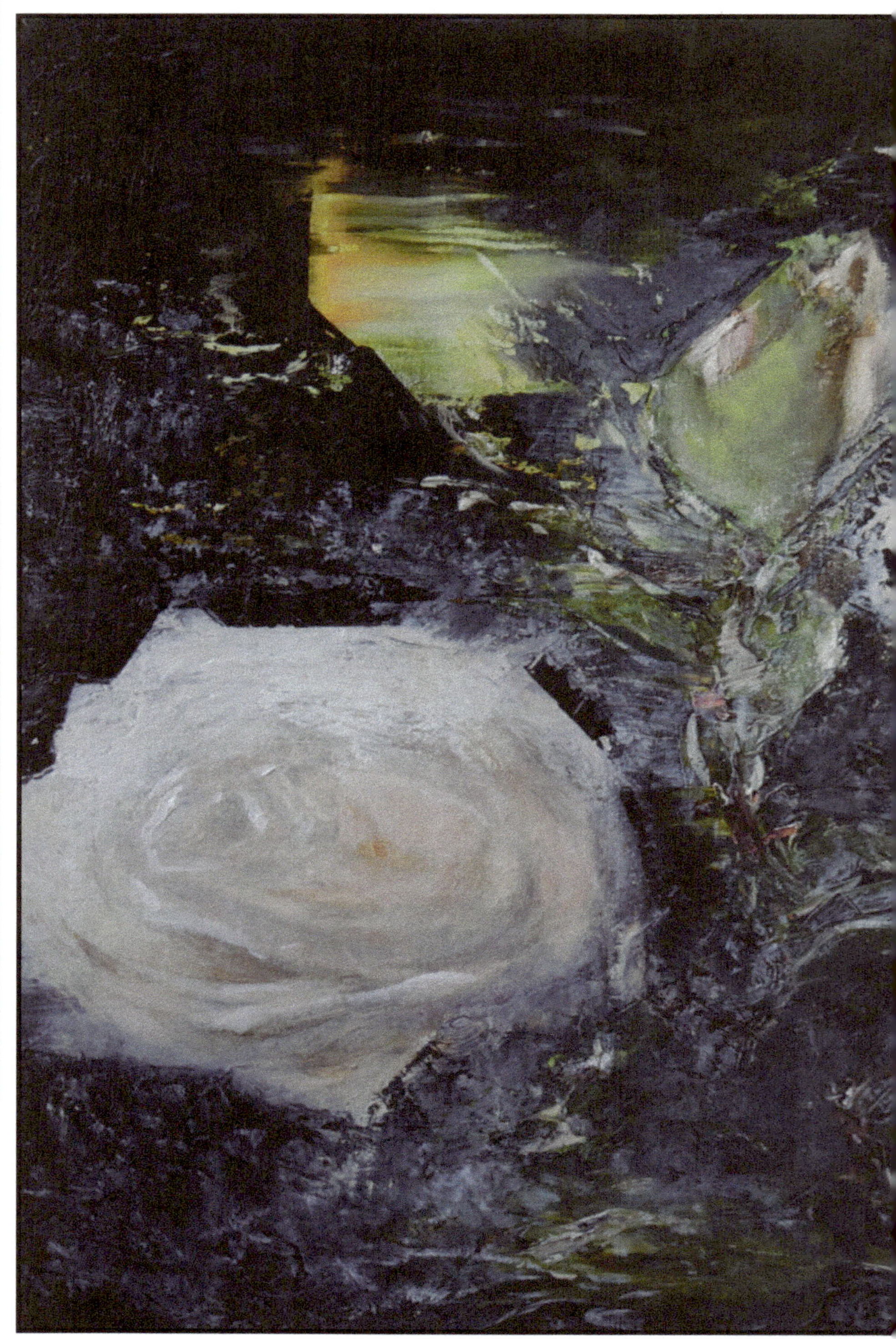

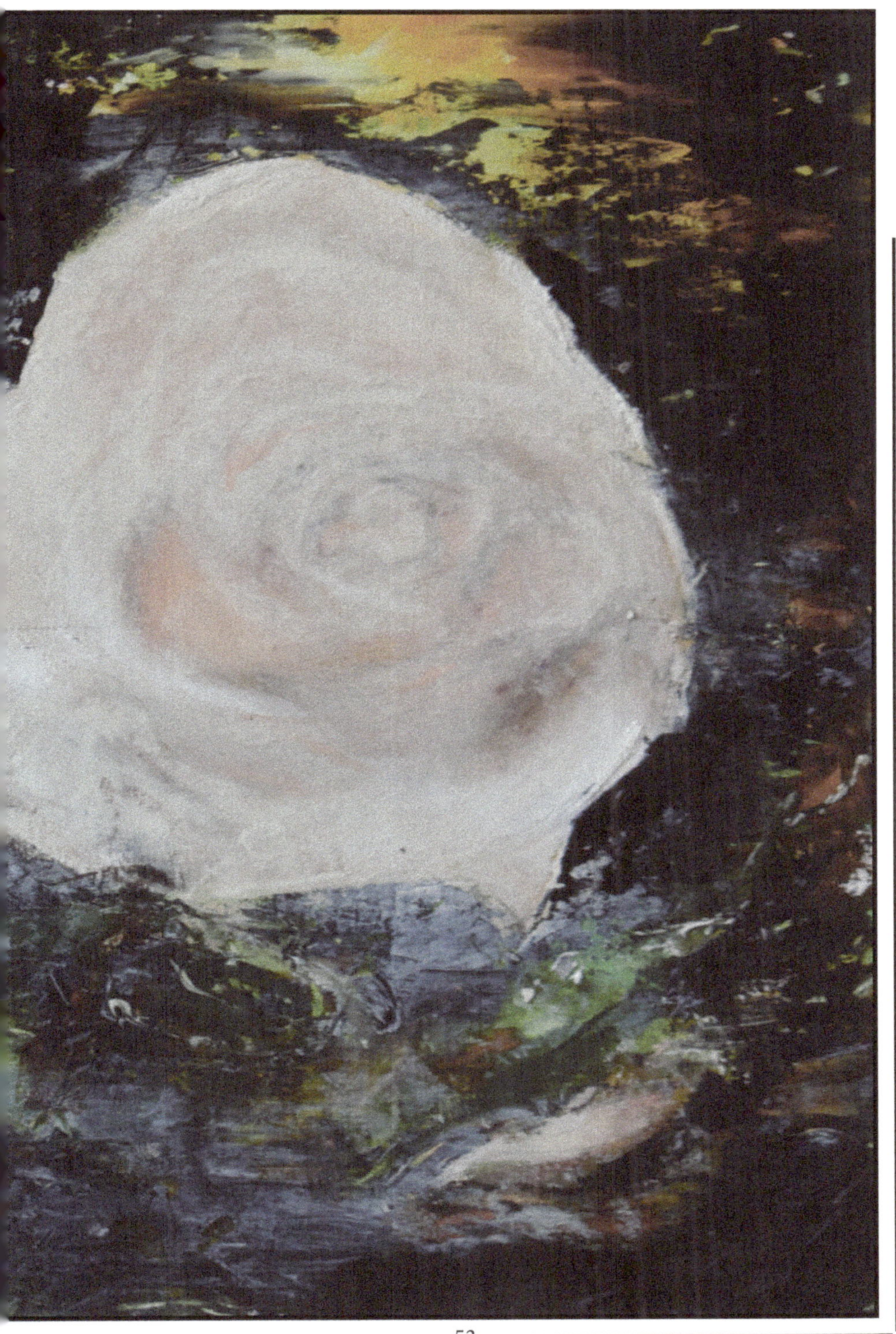

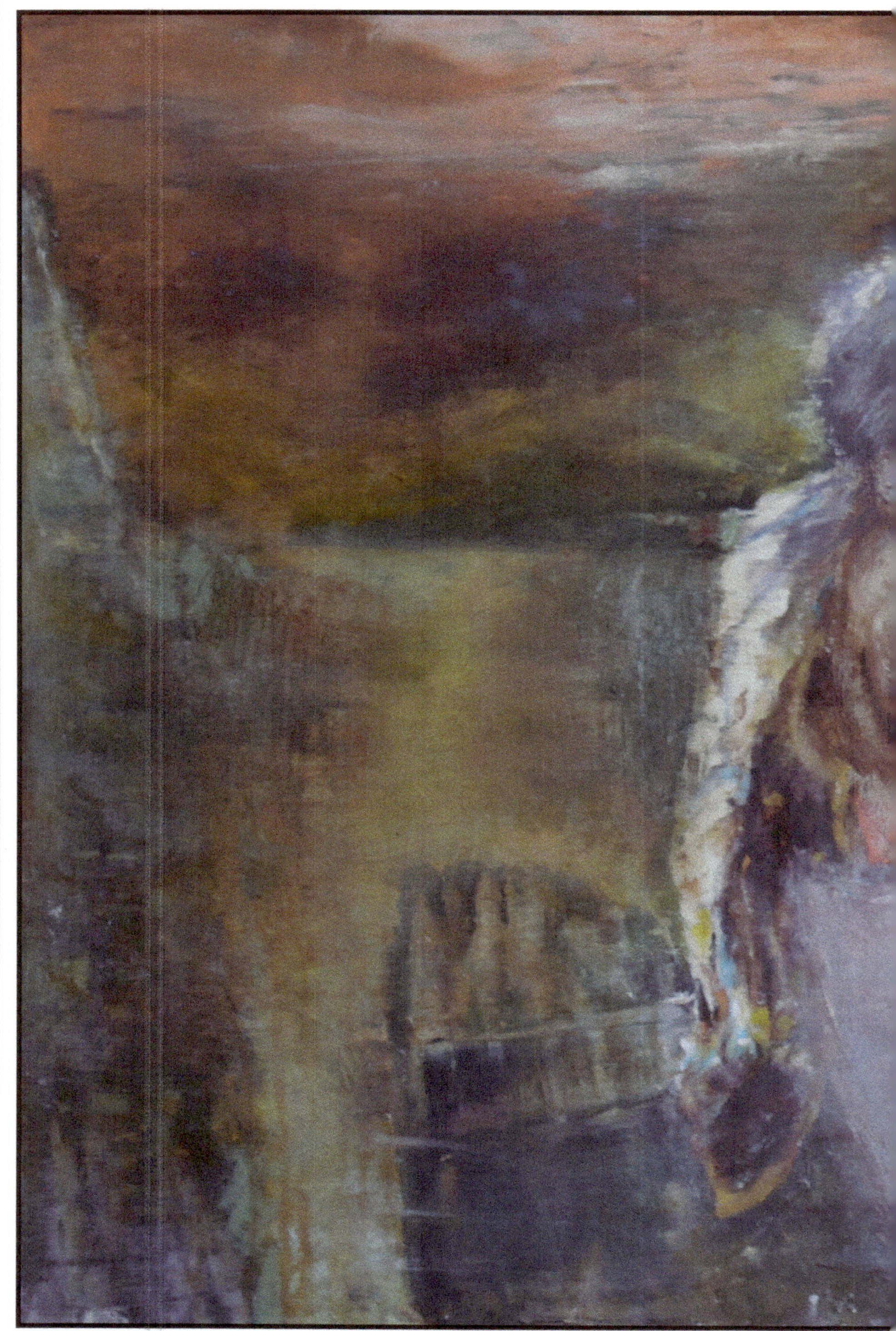

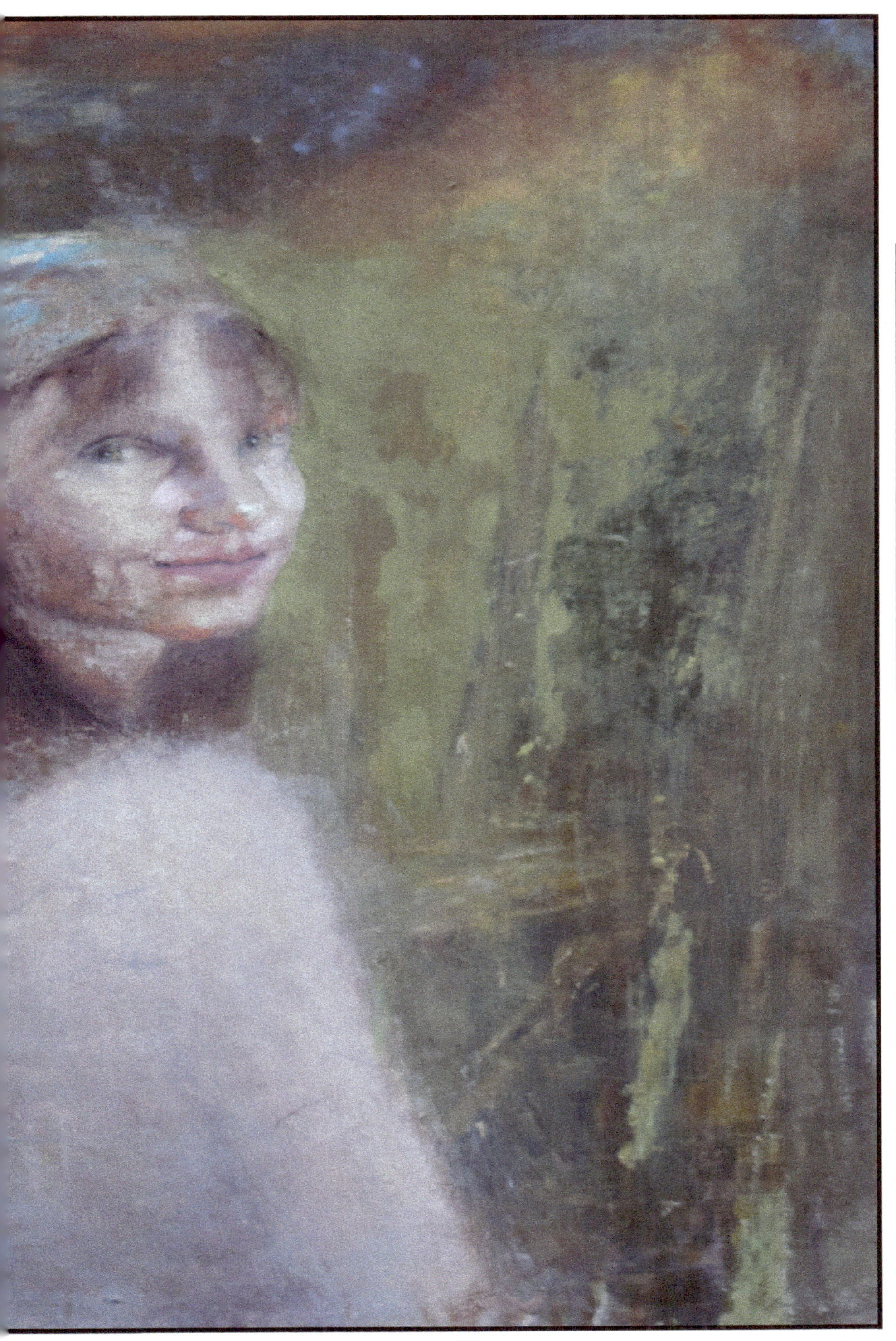

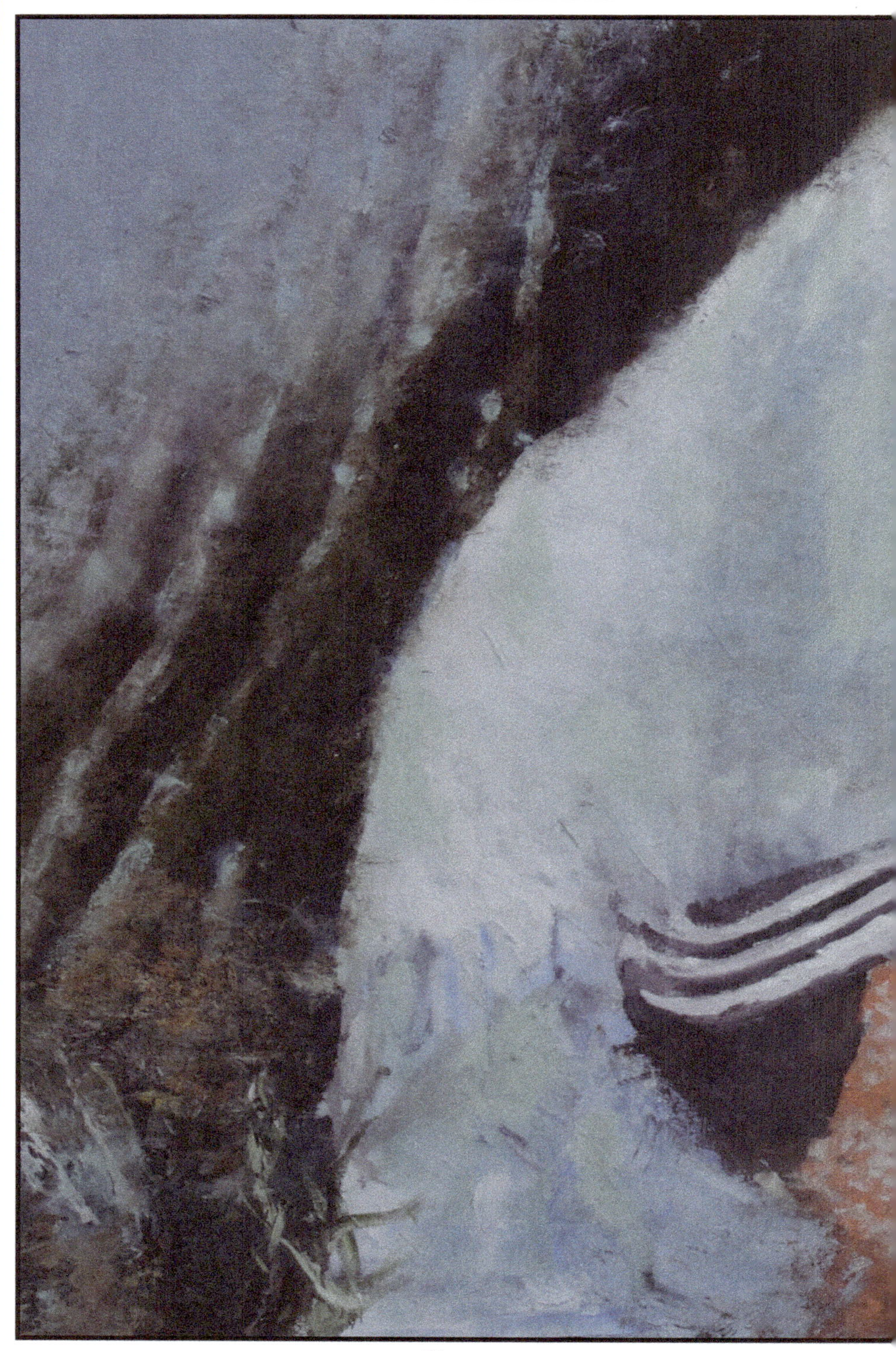

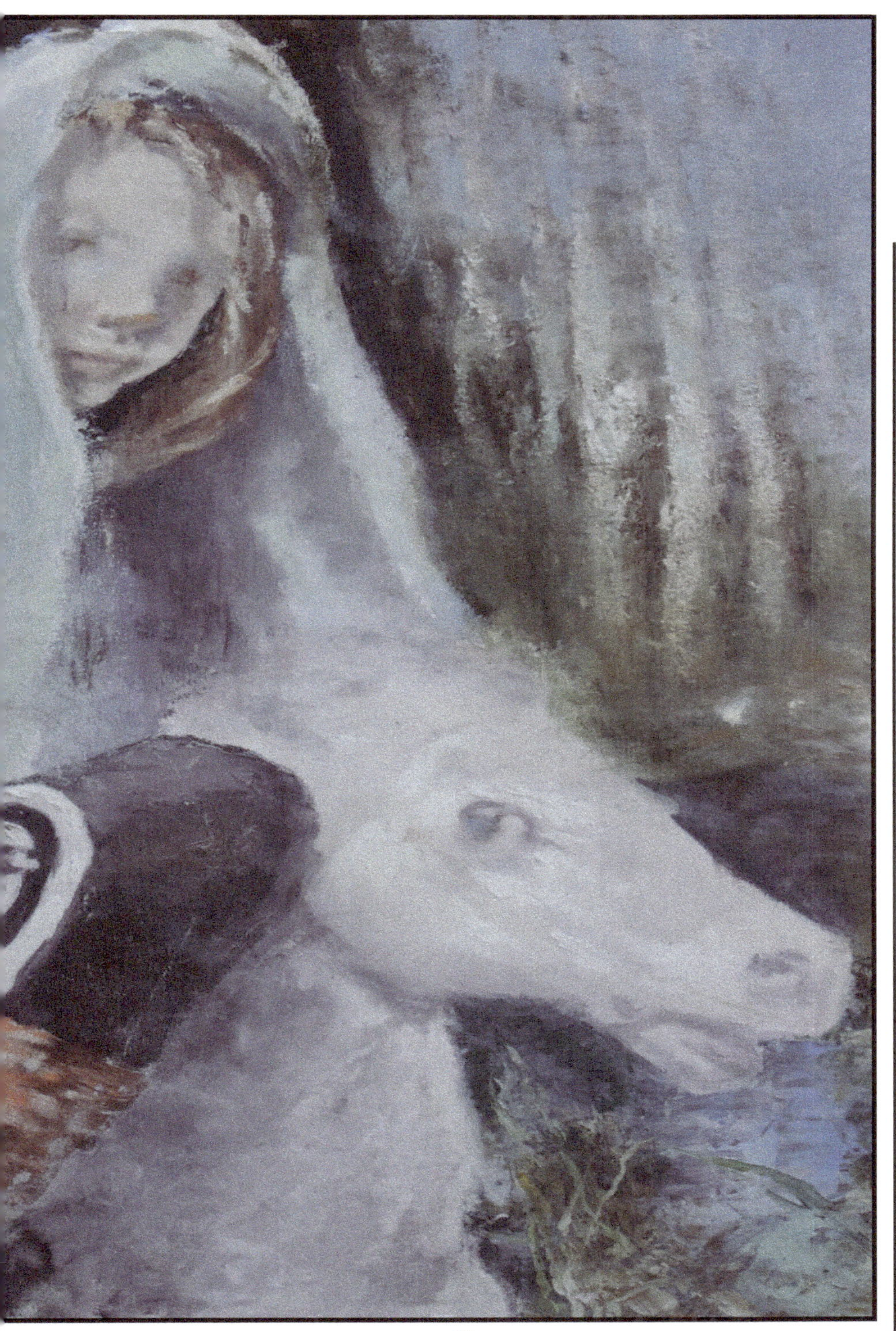

Invitations

Taylor Mallay

Smallest creak on the steps,
small labored breaths,
me at my desk, legs crossed and
listening to the high-pitched split tone
of the neighbor's saw — a jagged rhythm
criss-crossing with car doors slammed
in the warmth of a bright summer morning.

Thick grey fur brushes
the back of my bare calf.
I reach down, hold my hand limp
in front of two blue eyes — cold nose
pokes at my palm, pauses
and pushes against it.
Over the years, I've learned to wait openly
instead of calling her to me.

Thwack of a hammer
and we both startle —
echoed mumbles of made-up jumbles
of various expletives:
motherfu-go-dam-friggit!

My neighbor is repairing the fence
after yesterday's storm,
which swam through the air,
at first, with a sustained, low hum,
and then crashed through the streets
after tasting our atmosphere:
its pleasing mixture of sticky humidity
and cool twilight.

Scattered branches lay
in the wake of its daze — it stumbled by
with the swift arc of a burly man
drunk and delighted, made dangerous
by the simple fact of his weight
and gravity's existence.
There was no offering here,
only acceptance.

My neighbor sighs
and the hammering stops
for a moment.
Quiet steps move away from me,
quick as they came;
she slips out of my sight,
down the stairs, sure as a lioness
in her self-belonging.

The Art of Piercing

Rommel Chrisden Rollan Samarita

after Raman Bhardwaj

"He never understood the art

      of piercing," she said. The needle

is different from the needle

      -work. Swordwork and needlework

are never one. That is to say

      cutting her open is not the same

as piercing her. "Everything

      begins with the skin." So, the man

wounded her to conquer only

      her skin, her skin... not her being.

"He never understood the art

      of piercing," she said. What a man

opens, a woman closes. Like

      an open wound, or a history of pain...

"Piercing precedes pain. Often,

      when there is piercing; there is no pain."

This is how she discovered

      the thread and learned to sew her

wounds and stories gently.

      More than a woman's body, her art.

Circus Girl

Kat Hofland

I'm thinking of cutting my hair, of dying it a stilted purple, staining my eyes, turning them into bullet proof-glass, piercing my tongue, tattooing the Five of Swords onto my chest, cutting off my pinky finger, maybe my middle finger, too, carving a hole straight from the top of my foot to the bottom. I'm thinking of falling asleep in a garden, one that only grows Venus Flytraps, one that the sun can't find, one that's very far away from here, wherever that is. I'm going to strip myself into nothing, how about that? I'd ask you about it but you wouldn't answer, I'd call your name but I'm not sure I know it anymore, I'd look for you but I don't think it'd matter if I did. Do you have an opinion? I guess I'll dive right into the water, naked, just like you like me, just like I like myself. I want it to be cold. No, freezing. I want to become an icicle. My natural state, you would say. Rich, that's what you'd call it.

Living in a White World

Chad Murray

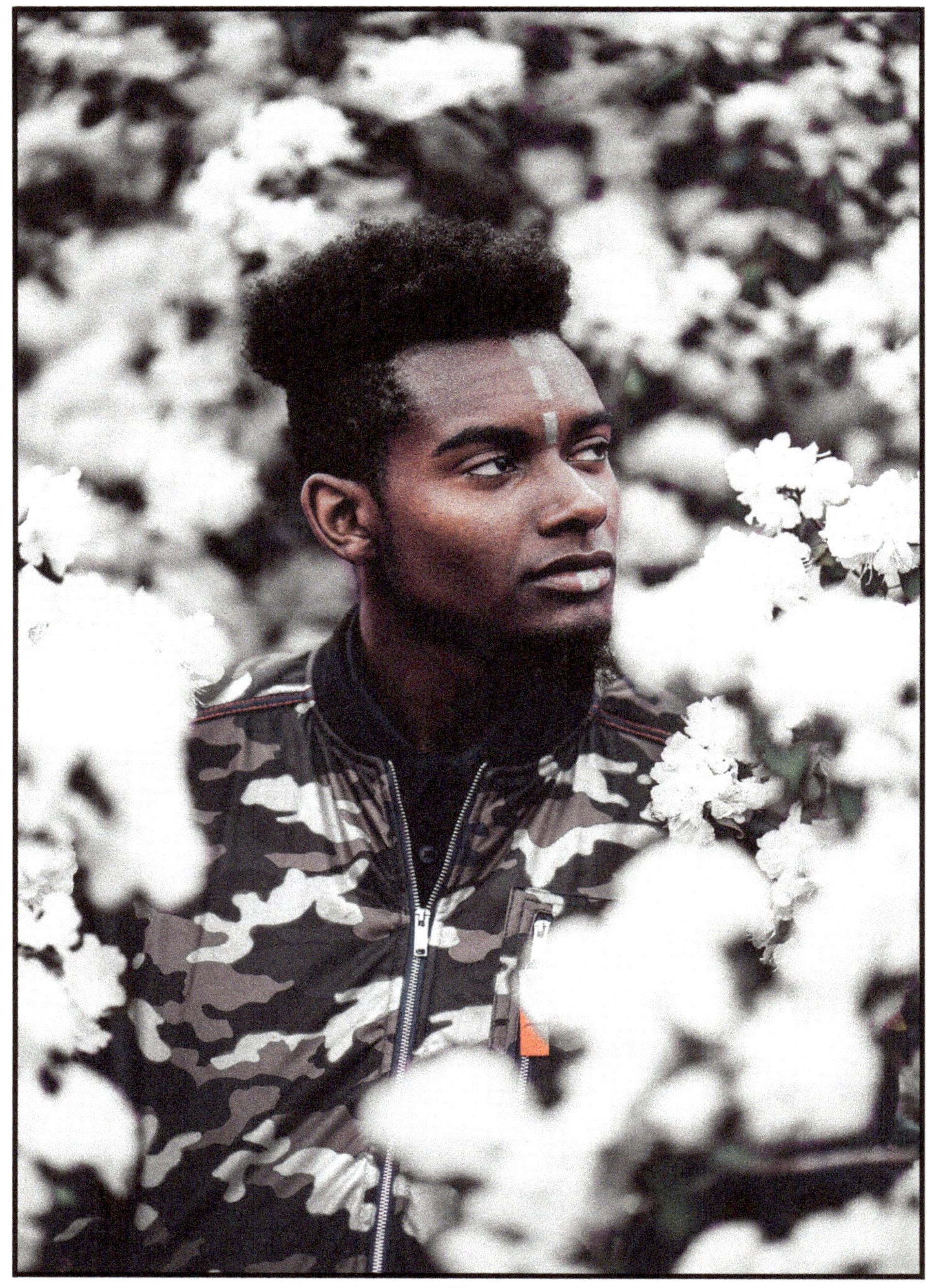

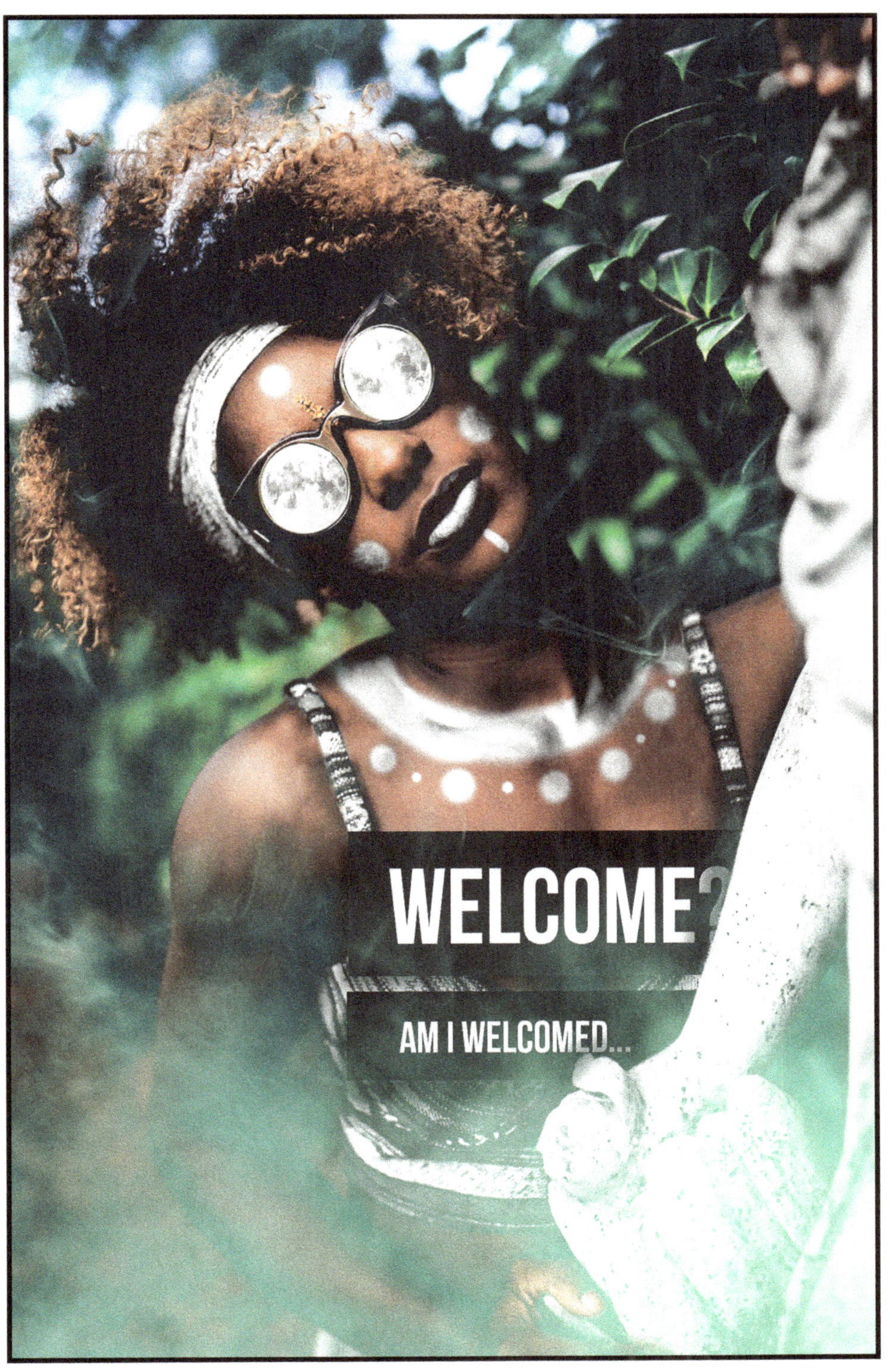

WELCOME?
AM I WELCOMED...

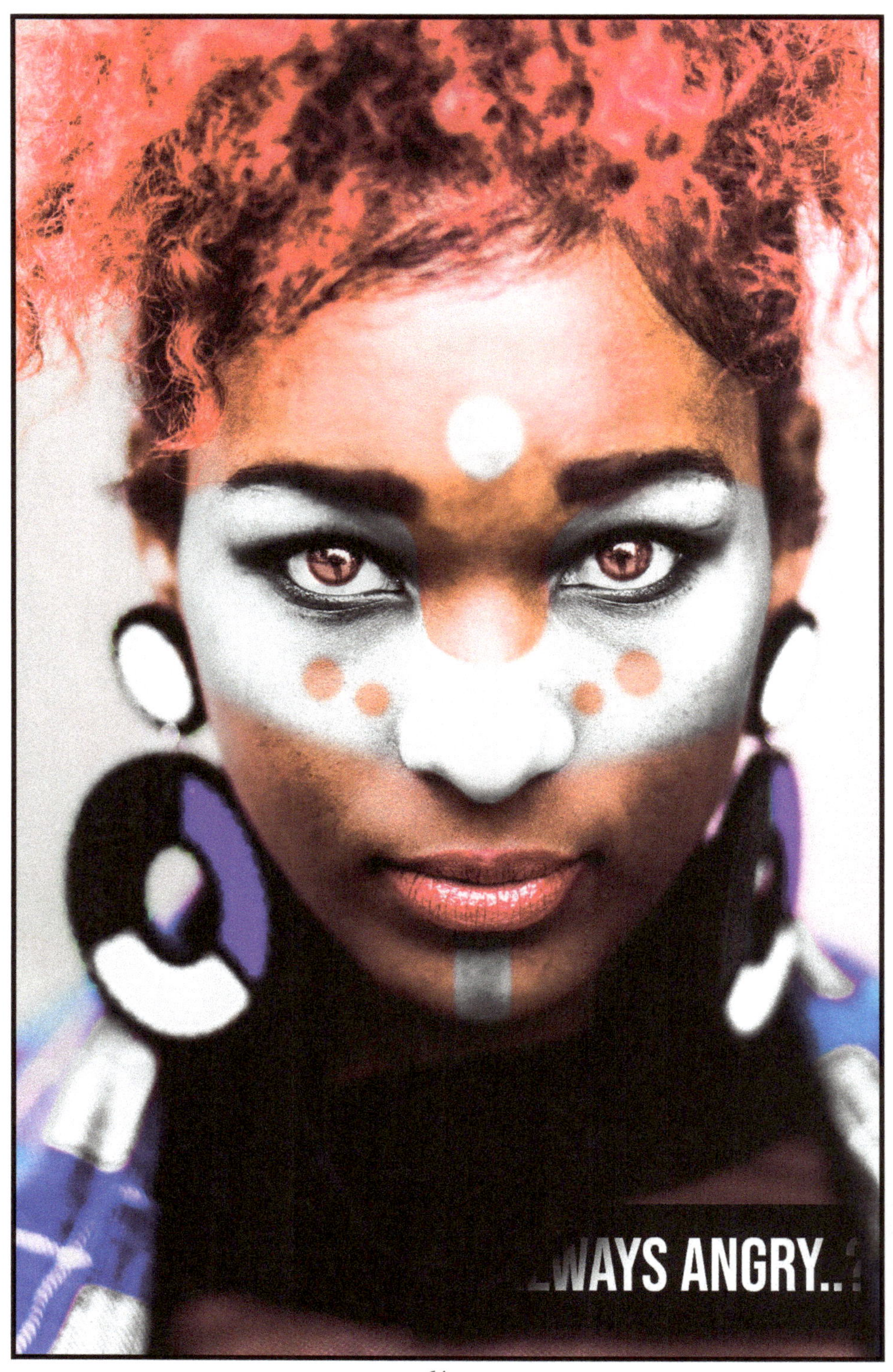

WAYS ANGRY...?

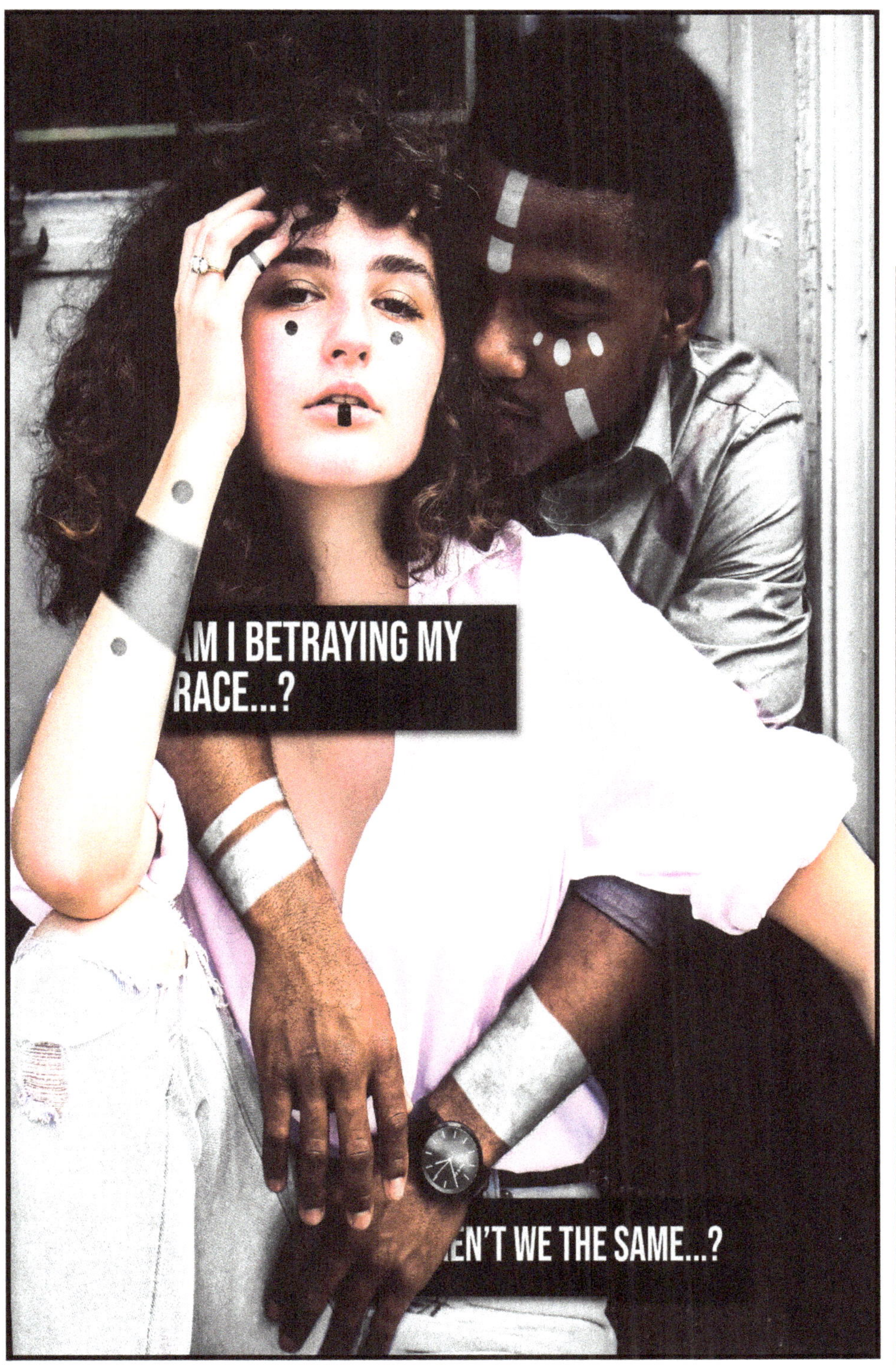
AM I BETRAYING MY RACE...?
EN'T WE THE SAME...?

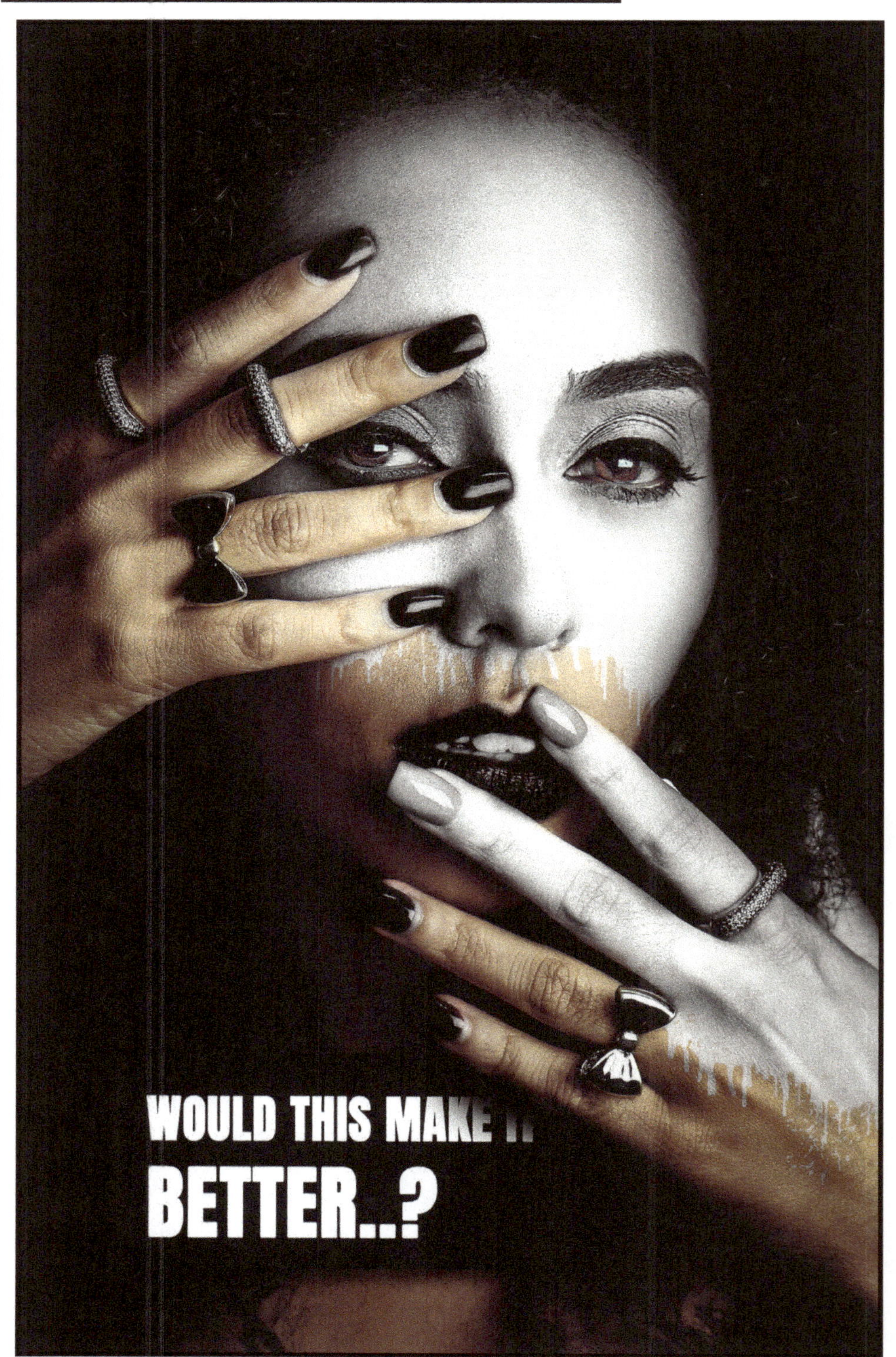

WOULD THIS MAKE IT
BETTER..?

Art Submission

Jason R. Montgomery

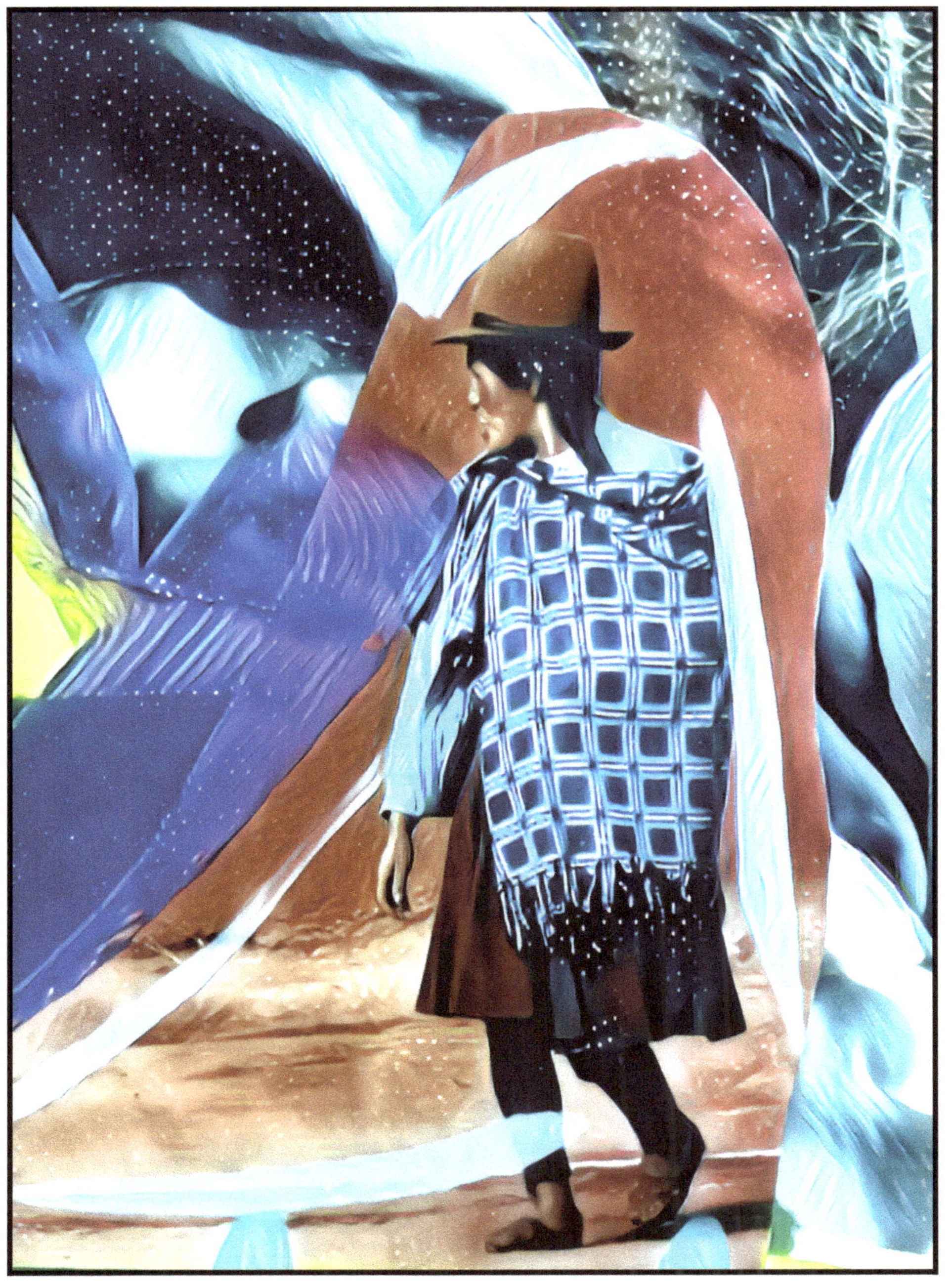

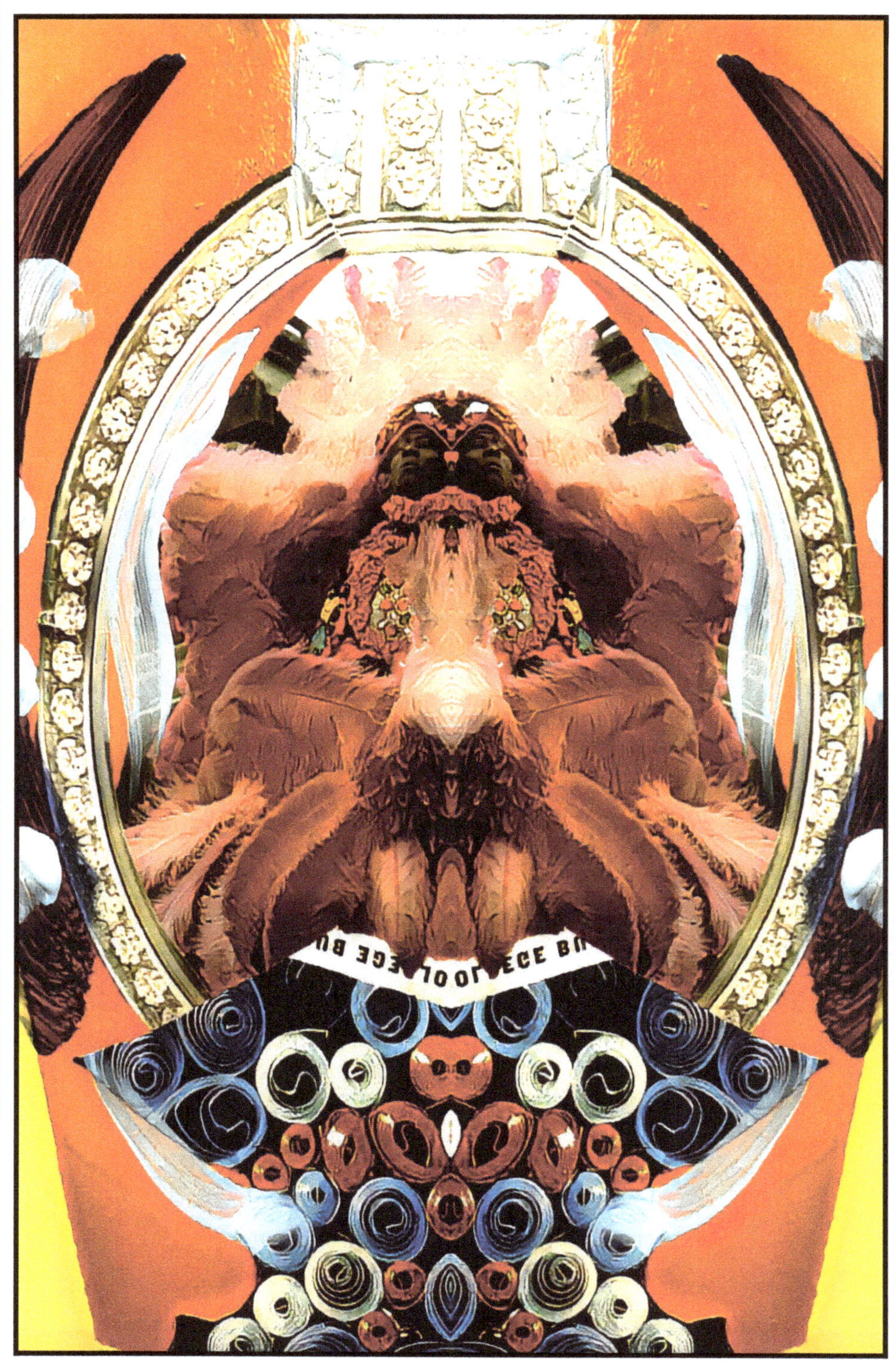

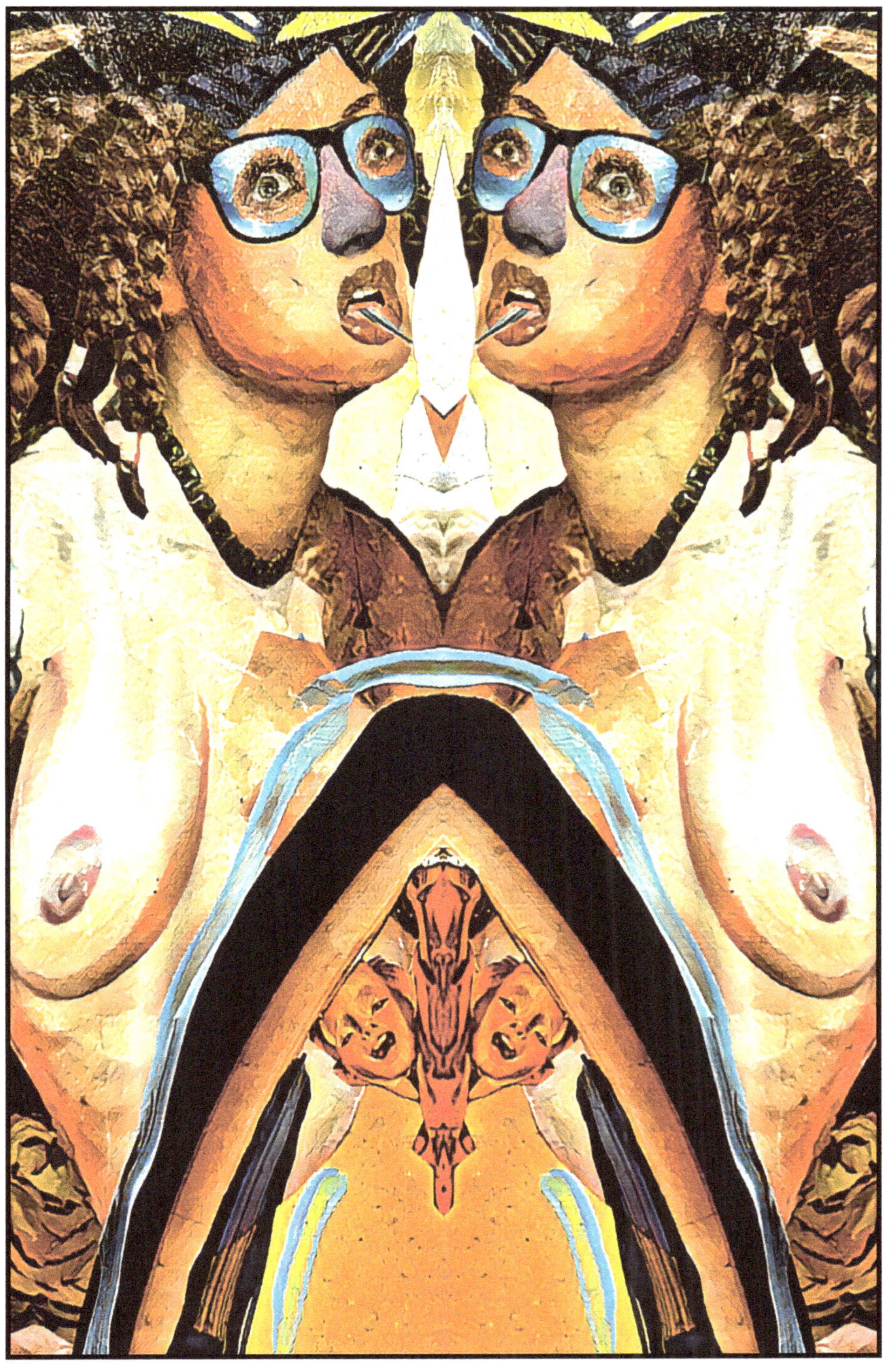

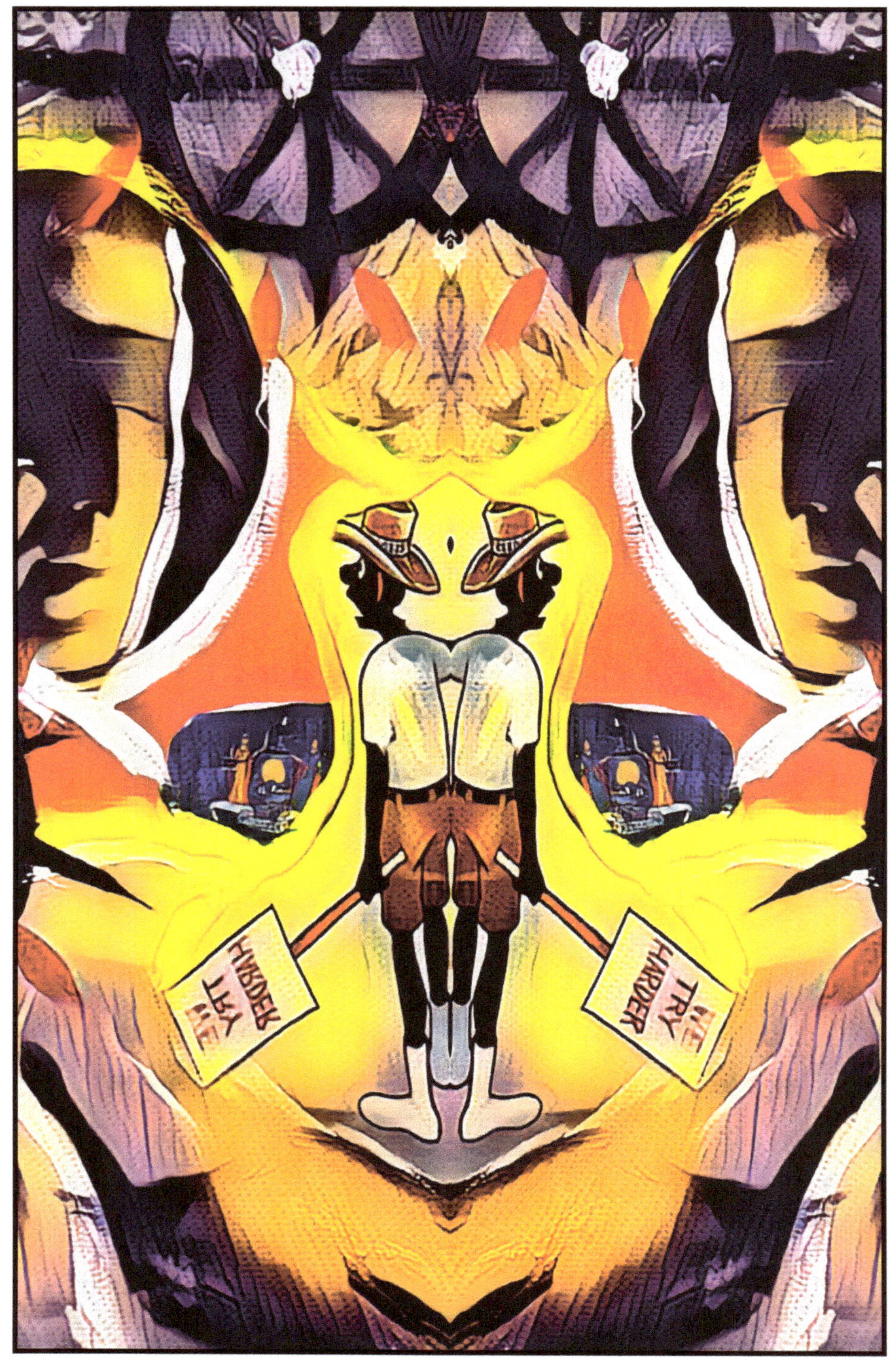
WE
TRY
HARDER

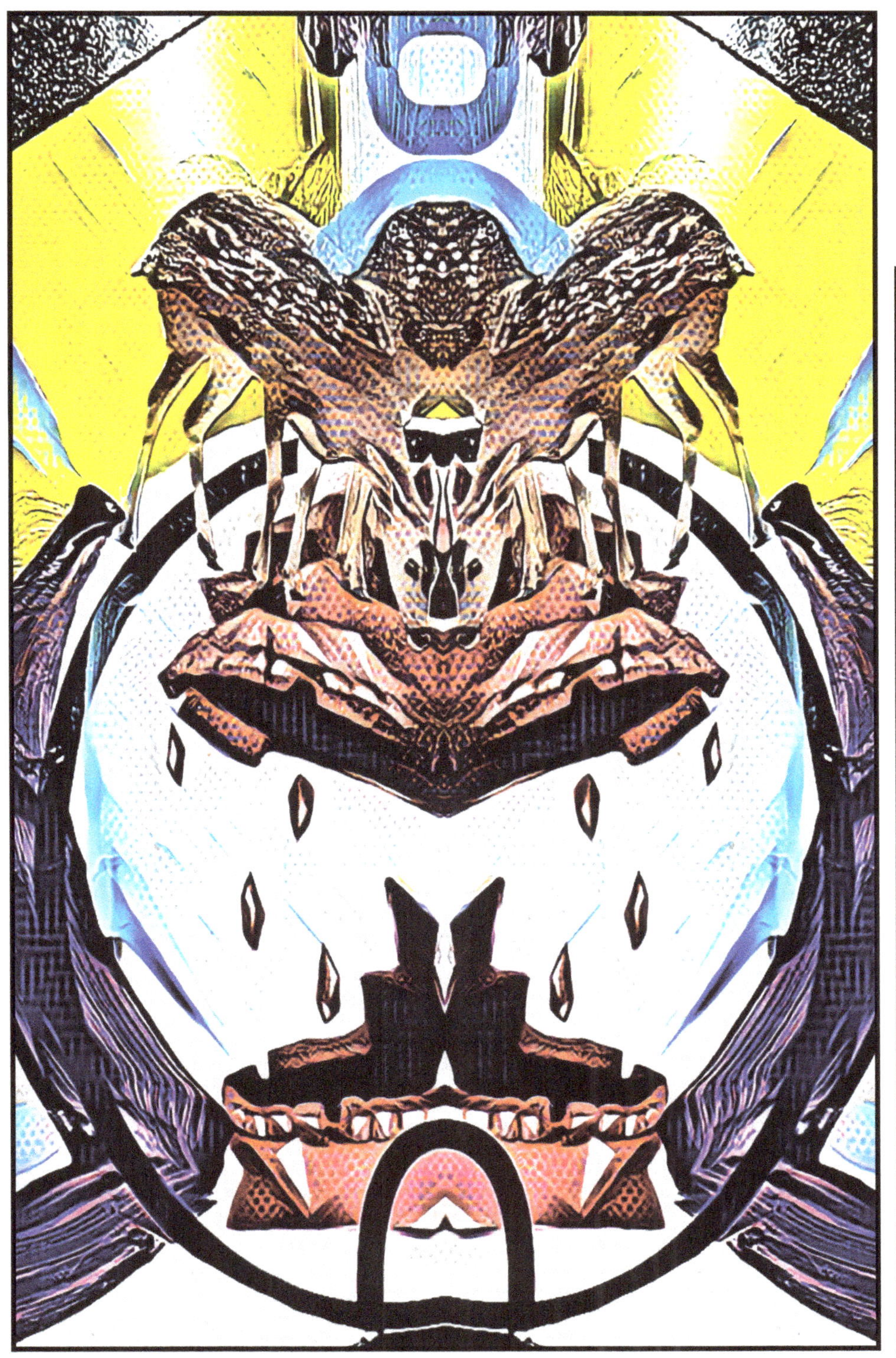

A Dangerous Game

Lily Rooks

This is satire. This essay will be satirical. Just so we're all clear. It is clear, isn't it?

I only ask because some people (although I wouldn't call Twitter users people), don't seem to understand that when I say Covid-19 is a made-up virus, invented by the government as an excuse to cancel Coachella because too many kids do drugs in the desert and because Frank Ocean's music is the soundtrack to the rebellion, that I'm joking.[1]

And when I say that you can kill the virus by making a "quaran-tini" mixed with vodka, diet coke, cumin, charcoal, rubbing alcohol, crushed up Advil, and yeast (left over from the bread you tried to bake), and then drink it while binge-watching episodes of *Grey's Anatomy*, that of course I don't mean it.[2]

Or when I claim that taking baths in lukewarm orange juice is a sure-fire way to protect against the disease, since many people have pointed out that the sun is effective in killing the virus, and Vitamin D is found in both the sun *and* in orange juice, that I don't mean you should stockpile Minute Maid on your next trip to the grocery store.[3]

Or that we shouldn't wear masks because Bill Gates and Microsoft are secretly embedding them with special fibers laced with a powerful chemical that infects the brain when inhaled, forcing victims to develop a penchant for tight-fitting yoga pants and organic grain bowls, and causing them to develop the urge to vote for Joe Biden[4]. It's all in jest.

You know I'm kidding, right? When I say that this virus was invented by Zoom as a way to force people indoors and onto virtual meetings and teleconferences. That they created this sickness in a lab and then injected it into GMO corn as a way to infect the world and drive up company stocks and promote the fun new Zoom backgrounds you can download on your computer.[5]

Please say you know I'm not being serious. Please tell me there's room for satire in this world, this world that already feels like one big joke. Although, to be fair, maybe it's dangerous even to pretend, to engage in the ridiculous, to dabble in hyperbole. Maybe a joke is the most dangerous thing of all.

---

[1] Although, to be fair, I have seen many people online claiming that this pandemic is fake, made-up, and bogus, so maybe it is dangerous to joke like this.

[2] Although, to be fair, I have seen many people online downing bleach and pumping it into their bodies at the suggestion of the President, so maybe it is dangerous to joke like this.

[3] Although, to be fair, I have seen throngs of people outside, squashed up and close together, jockeying for some of the sun and natural light that is supposedly the cure for coronavirus (according to the President). I've also seen some unfortunate results of tanning bed fever, since apparently applying "light and heat" is the solution, so maybe it is dangerous to joke like this.

[4] Although, to be fair, I have seen many people online seriously claiming that Bill Gates predicted this disease in 2015 and that he and Melinda have been testing a vaccine on poor children in India and that they are using this pandemic as a way to implant the public with microchips, so maybe it is dangerous to joke like this.

[5] Although, to be fair, I have seen many people claim, both online and in town halls, that Covid-19 is caused by radiation from 5-G towers, which were set up as a way to "depopulate" the earth, so maybe it is dangerous to joke like this.

Donuts at the Fair, and the Banality of a Sweet Tooth

Will McDonald

"You ever worked a fryer before, kid?" Dave asked me. Mid-30s, apathetic and reeking of last night's bad decisions, Dave was my boss at my first real job. I was a carnie, working the mini-donuts stand at the Minnesota State Fair. I was 16 and needed the money to cover my growing reliance on Proactiv acne cream.

"N-no." I said clumsily. "I don't think so?"

"Well it's hot, so if you screw up you'll burn yourself."

With one hand Dave took the fry basket and garnered a horde of raw donuts. He held the basket over the bubbling fryer.

"Frying donuts ain't all that different than boiling lobster."
What a confusing analogy. What the hell did donuts have in common with boiling lobster?

"You just scoop 'em up…and you dunk them in… like this."

Dave lowered the fry basket, filled with donuts, into the hot fryer. He wore a hat, and the hair on the sides of his head was greasy and starting to gray. When he stretched his arms forward I could see under his aged t-shirt a dimming Celtic Knot tattooed on his bicep. From the little that I knew about him, Dave was not a happy man. He growled more often than he spoke and operated as if he could work the entire booth asleep—which one could easily be mistaken for thinking. His shoulders perpetually slouched, and nearly every third sentence was interrupted by a yawn.

Distracted by his stench, assumedly the Windsor he had drowned himself in last night, I looked away from the fryer, holding my breath and concentrating on my blurred reflection in the stainless-steel service counter so I didn't have to face his odor head on.

Out of my periphery, I could see the dough goodies submerge into the boiling fryer fluid, followed by a faint, yet high-pitched shriek. In my distraction and attempt to shield myself from Dave's basement floor cologne, I couldn't figure out where the shriek was coming from until it was drowned out by the escalation of the "sizzling" coming from the fryer.

"Ya got it?" Dave asked me, unaware I hadn't paid attention to anything he had just done.

"Yeah... I got it."

"Okay, don't mess it up. It's literally the easiest damn job in the world."

Dave walked away, yawning as he turned from me. I stood at the fryer and slowly put my gloves on. I grabbed a clean basket with one hand, and the side of the pan holding all the raw donuts in the other. I scooped a basketful and moved it towards the fryer. As I held it above the bubbling oil I heard a voice cry, "No! Please! Please don't kill us!" It was small and high pitched. I looked all around to see where it was coming from.

"Here! Down here!" It cried again.

"Wh-who said that?" I asked as I spun my head around 360 degrees.

"Us!" The voice was beneath me.

I looked down at the basket I was holding over the hot fryer.

"Yes, us! The innocent victims of your gluttonous massacres!" The donuts were the ones screaming.

"You're... alive?" I was stunned.

In a similarly high-pitched voice another donut, much less patient and more confrontational than the other, screamed at me. "Yes, we're alive! Did you not hear your merciless, barroom chump of an overlord? We cook just like lobsters —ALIVE, in this murderous bath of stewing vegetable oils!"

I quickly learned that Dave's analogy was not as confusing or misguided as I initially thought. The donuts informed me that not only were they alive when cooked—let alone sentient—they also mate in the missionary position and have lifespans up to 100 years when not prematurely interrupted by a predator's sweet tooth.

The donut who first caught my attention pleaded with me. "Don't kill us! We lock eyes during sex!"

I turned to look and see if anyone was around me. If anyone was hearing the same things I was. This couldn't be happening!

"This acne cream must be seeping into my brain... I'm losing my mind..." I uttered aloud.

The second donut retorted. "It's not the acne cream you pock-marked, homicidal yokel! We are alive and speaking to you, and it's best you believe it, man!"

The first donut continued arguing his case for clemency. "We live, we breathe, we make love..."

"We abide by an electoral college system!" The second donut chimed in again.

"Yes," The first agreed. "Again, he's right. Even in our flaws we are similar!"

Every sentiment of reality I held had been shattered in a matter of moments. I was so overwhelmed with perplexity that I had failed to notice a customer had made his way to the service window. "Hello?" The customer addressed me.

Still legitimizing his kind to me, the second donut continued. "We drive cars, visit tanning salons, beat up paparazzi..."

"Yes, yes, we are similar even in our ugliness as well as our beauty," The first donut interjected. "I don't know how that's helping our plea for mercy. But surely, pubescent friend, you must have mercy?"

"Hello?!" The customer was angry. Could he not hear the sentient dough that was begging for its preservation on the other side of the counter?

"H-hello, Sir. How may I help you?" I mustered up.

"I'd like to buy some mini-donuts. One bag please."

"Umm...okay. One second. Coming right up."

Upon hearing the above transaction take place, the second donut agonized, "Our doom has found its predator! Alas, it has come to this hyperglycemial ruin. Father Duncan, please... begin the Last Rites."

A timid voice with an Irish accent began from within the basket. "Our *Fodder*, who art in Heaven, hallowed be thy name..."

Again, the first donut pleaded. "You, mustn't! Please, you mustn't. For I know you are not some Jacobin. You are kind. A kind man, you are, yes?"

Beads of sweat tumbled down my forehead and I began to feel a knot in my stomach. How did I find myself here holding the guillotine's rope? I took this job to make some money, learn responsibility, and get my parents off my back. This was the most morally embattled I had ever been. But, as many had told me before, hard work pays off, and this was certainly going to be hard. And work wasn't supposed to be fun or easy, anyways. My job was to fry donuts, whether I liked it or not.

"I...I don't want to hurt anyone. I'm just doing my job!"

"So was Eichmann!" Cried the second donut in immediate response.

Dammit! What a gut-shot!

"No!" I defended. "That's not fair! I just really need the money!"

The first donut, realizing his defeat, began a morbid, rhythmic monologue.

> "Ah, so that is but the truest and only reason for our scorched fate:
> the triumph of the merchant. Damned are we the honorable, for
> greed shall be the knife in our side, just as it was the treacherous
> Brutus' dagger in the great Caesar's. May your pockets, brigand,
> be lined with the most minimal of wages, soaked in the invisble,
> sugary blood of our kind! And your villainy—with the likes of
> Gloucester and Machiavelli it shall rival!"

The customer's voice boomed over the service counter. "C'mon, kid! Hurry it up!"

Hearing the man's impatience, Dave turned the corner, looking as if he had just been woken up. "I'm sorry, sir." He said to the customer. "Is something the matter?"

"Yeah, as a matter of fact there is! I've been waiting on this kid forever."

"Let's go, kid!" Dave barked. "Get the guy his damn donuts!"

The sweat continued to pour down my forehead, and the knots tied tighter in my stomach. My back tensed up as my mind deliberated at a rate of a million thoughts per second what my next course of action would be.

Beneath me, the quiet voice of Father Duncan prayed, "Merciless *Jaysus*, who at the hour of thy sacred passion..."

The second donut, having accepted his fate, approached death with spontaneity, making love, face-to-face, with another.

The first donut was now huddled in a corner with two others, one a tearful lover, the other a smaller, confused confectionary, clutched to the larger donut's mid-section. Before turning his head into his two loved ones, he shouted out into the open air, "Remember us, brethren of dough! On this day remember us, we few, we happy few, we band of brothers!"

"I'm only doing my job." I whispered as I closed my eyes. My head hanged low. "I'm only doing my job…"

I plunged the basket into the fryer. The same shriek I heard before echoed below me before the sound of the sizzle drowned it out, once again.

Tears rushed down my face as I raised the basket of donuts out of the fryer and dumped their doughy corpses into a paper bag. I sprinkled sugar over the bag and handed it to the customer. I accepted his cash and put it in the register's tray. Upon looking up, another face appeared before me.

"Can you get me a bag of mini-donuts please?" They said.

I wiped the tears from my pimpled cheeks. "Of course. That's my job."

Immaculate Conception

Art by Andrea Jones

Words by Sonya Burke

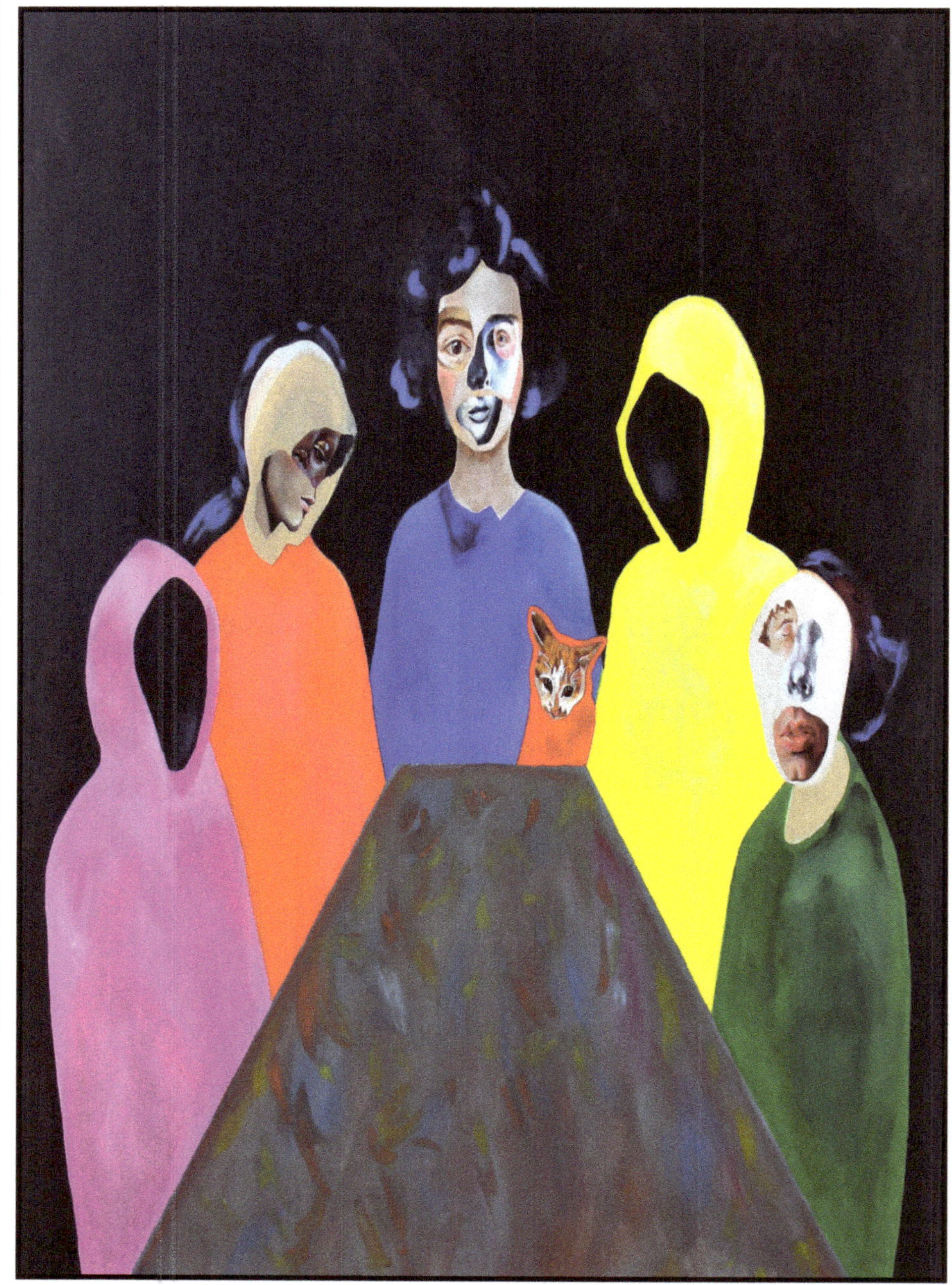

Why we might meet once a year to
Bring ourselves to the table, dead parts
And all, towing our loads which
We have each taught each other to carry
I don't know. Harder still, we must
Pretend to be the same people,
Some of us, not naming names,
Must pretend to be people.

This year the feast has already been eaten,
By an animal higher on the food chain,
And though I will not be there bent
under my own weight to see it,
I can see the emptiness if I close one eye,
The one with the scar of immaculate
Conception.

In Order Of Appearance:

Andy Kerstetter is a queer poet, journalist and freelance writer living in Idaho's Wood River Valley. He has worked for newspapers and magazines since earning a degree in writing in 2010 from Geneva College in western Pennsylvania, where he was born and raised. His poetry so far has appeared in Gravitas and Sixfold, and his debut collection, "The Inferno Lessons," is forthcoming from Kattywompus Press.

Sarah Bricault has a PhD in neurobiology and currently works as a postdoc. Her poetry is influenced by her struggles with depression and anxiety as well as her fascination with how the mind and the body come into being.

Chris Foster is a poet living in Tucson, Arizona. His work has previously appeared in Adelaide Magazine, the Scarlet Leaf Review, and the California Quarterly.

Laurie Philip Michaels creates original drawings of women that highlight their diversity and beauty. She hopes these works will evoke an emotional reaction in you. She says, "the hostile way that images of women are produced and consumed is challenged by my work."
As you look through Ms. Michaels' list of influences, she worries you might be puzzled that her work doesn't fall neatly into any of these artist's styles, or into their associated movements. She was deeply affected by each of these artists or movements, but did not aspire to follow in their footsteps as a craftsman might. Instead, each influence informs her aesthetic sensibility as she tries to create something new, fresh, and relevant.
Of her influences, the one she's most commonly compared to is Patrick Nagel, a Los Angeles pop artist from the 1970s and 80s, who did stark, very commercial, very slick images of vaguely detached, vaguely Asian, vaguely sophisticated women, sexually intimidating and fierce. Her intention, however, is unlike Nagel. She says, "Nagel specifically intended to objectify his subject. I want to personalize and humanize our vision of women. Nagel didn't want to know the women he imagined in his works. I want you to feel you already know my subjects. I want you to recognize yourself in them and want to meet them."
Laurie Philip Michaels studied at El Camino College, Torrance, CA, CSU Dominguez Hills in Carson, CA, and The Evergreen State College in Olympia, WA, but her art is the result of her personal journey and not formal training.
Influences
Chinese ink wash, Japanese wood block, stencil street art, Pablo Picasso, Andy Warhol, Vincent Van Gogh, Claude Monet, Greek Pottery, Roman Statuary, Cycladic Art, Salvador Dali, Man Ray, Patrick Nagel, Ballet

Emily Benson writes poems of humanity, longing, and nature. She lives in Western New York with her husband and two sons. Ms. Benson has previously been published in The Esthetic Apostle, Unstamatic, and Hey, I'm Alive Magazine.

Brandyce Ingram is a writer and jazz-head in Austin, Texas. Her work has appeared in The Esthetic Apostle, The Austin Chronicle, Sand Hills Literary Magazine, OxMag, Cathexis Northwest Press, The Write Launch, and elsewhere. She thinks Jupiter is the lovable, drunk (and gassy) uncle of the galaxy and Lisa Simpson should be president.

Michelle Geoga is a writer and artist from Chicago with an MFAW from The School of the Art Institute and a recipient of a Yaddo residency. You can find their work in Five on the Fifth, Longleaf Review, Cleaver, New American Paintings, Storm Cellar and forthcoming in Bridge Eight.

Clara Mendoza is a high school student who runs her school's creative writing club and literary magazine.

Paul Ilechko is the author of the chapbooks "Bartok in Winter" (Flutter Press) and "Graph of Life" (Finishing Line Press). His work has appeared in a variety of journals, including Juxtaprose, As It Ought To Be, Cathexis Northwest Press, Inklette and Pithead Chapel. He lives with his partner in

Lambertville, NJ.

Ciarán Ó Gríofa lives in Limerick City, Ireland.

Turner Hilliker is a visual artist, illustrator, and designer from Northern Virginia. He received his MFA in Book Arts and Printmaking from the University of the Arts in Philadelphia, Pennsylvania. He is currently exploring layered narratives in his work.

Ann-Marie Brown is a Canadian artist working on the west coast of B.C. on a property she shares with her husband, son, dog, and the occasional bear. Her oil & encaustic paintings have been exhibited across the United States & Canada, and have found their way into public, private & corporate collections.

Taylor Mallay is a student from MI who enjoys hiking and old movies.

Rommel Chrisden Rollan Samarita is an M.A. Candidate of the Department of Literature at De La Salle University, Manila, Philippines. He is the author of "There, in Folded Space, We Must Have Met,' Artist's Choice winner in Rattle's Ekphrastic Challenge. He researches contemporary Philippine writing, modern American poetry, and their conceptual intersections.

Kat Hofland is a writer based out of Phoenix, Arizona. She graduated from Arizona State University with a degree in Public Policy. She is a co-founder of Rinky Dink Press, and her work has been featured in Write On, Downtown; Light; Little Somethings Press; and Insight II from Four Chambers Press.

Chad Murray is a Graphic Design and Visual Artist that is pursuing a career in the arts. Ever since he was a child he has always thought of his ideal job as doing something with his hands. No matter what he does as long as he is creating he is happy. So his passion as an artist is to create and create as much work as he can until this world is just a little prettier than when he came in it.

Jason R. Montgomery, or JRM, is a Chicano/Indigenous Californian writer, painter, and playwright from El Centro, California. He merges Indigenous Californian and Chicano designs and aesthetics to explore the history of US colonization while synthesizing a decolonized motif that honors the complicated heritage of the postcolonial subject. www.attackbearpress.com

Lily Rooks graduated from New York University and lives on the East Coast. Her writing has been published in Chaleur Magazine, Spires Intercollegiate Literary Magazine, and Brio Literary Journal, and her award-winning poetry has been featured at The Grey Art Gallery in New York City. In her spare time, she likes to paint, watch nature documentaries, and explore the four corners of her living room.

Will McDonald is a comedy writer based in Minneapolis. Previously published satire on WhatThe-FussNews.com.

Andrea Jones lives in Liverpool, England and for the last nine years has taught art in prison. Andrea has had her artwork published in Pikchur Magazine, Average Art magazine, Wotisart Magazine, Candy Floss magazine, Thought Art Magazine, Envision Arts Magazine and Art Hole Magazine. She has exhibited her artwork in galleries and as part of The Beatles exhibition in Liverpool. Andrea was commissioned by Go Penguins to be a part of an art trail in Liverpool. The artwork featured on the front cover of Go Penguins Souvenir Guide which sold in Tate Liverpool and featured in newspapers in India and Toronto. Andrea also works as a promotional photographer for City Entertainment Group which is a theatre company based in Liverpool.

Sonya Burke is a writer, painter, textile puppet maker, and costumer. She grew up in rural Colorado and currently resides in Santa Fe, NM. She's completed two artist residencies and produced two creative process workshops for children in Tanzania and Bolivia. Her patchwork resume betrays an unusual array of skills typical of a zealous self-educator: carpentry, live performance, baking, and whitewater raft-guiding.

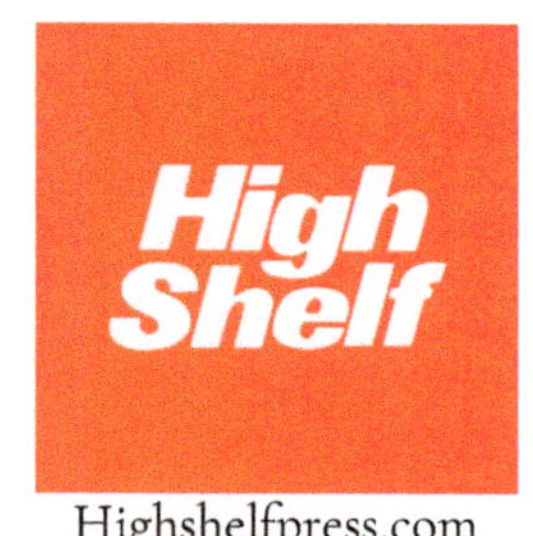

Highshelfpress.com